MW01282638

The Detour
An Off-Road Safari

Patricia McGregor

PRESS

Copyright © 2010 by Patricia McGregor

The Detour
An Off-Road Safari
by Patricia McGregor

Printed in the United States of America

ISBN 9781615799503

All rights reserved solely by the author. The author guarantees all contents are original and do not infringe upon the legal rights of any other person or work. No part of this book may be reproduced in any form without the permission of the author. The views expressed in this book are not necessarily those of the publisher.

Unless otherwise indicated, Bible quotations are taken from The NIV Study Bible. Copyright © 1985 by Zondervan Corporation, Grand Rapids, MI.

Cover Photo
Near Marsabit, Northern Kenya, on the "highway" between Cape Town and Cairo.
Photo Credit: Rev. Dr. Ian Montgomery

Typesetting, layout and design by
Xulon Press

www.xulonpress.com

OUTLINE

In memory and honor of the late
Rt. Rev. William Waqo.
Date of Birth – July 13, 1962
Date of Death – April 10, 2006

I dedicate this to his wife, Naomi who was also taken on an
off-road safari. May you find strength from God
for the journey.

ACKNOWLEDGEMENTS

A s in our whole lives and ministry, the people who helped this book come to print are like a patchwork quilt, each person sewing a part. Jesus is the tread which ties us all together. I would like to thank:

Our support team, churches, individuals and the People Reaching People Board who keep us on the mission field by their administrational tasks, communication and newsletter release, generous donations, and prayer support.

Our Kenyan friends and co-workers, who gave us the opportunity to serve them at St. Julian's Centre and for working in partnership with the Anglican Church of Kenya.

Polly Montgomery, Kara Schaffler, Jeannie Phillips, Cindy Fay and Phil Johnson for editing, reviewing the pre-press copy and offering valuable suggestions.

All those whose writings have been cited in this book.

Rev. Dr. Ian Montgomery for the front cover photo. The image was taken near Marsabit, Northern Kenya, on the "highway" between Cape Town and Cairo.

And to my husband, Todd, and my lovely daughters, Corbi and Charese who are a constant support.

Most of all, I acknowledge God, to whom I lift this pilgrimage prayer:

O Lord Jesus Christ, You are the Way, the Truth and the Life. Grant to us who tread in Your earthly footsteps, a sense of awe, wonder and holiness. May our hearts burn within us as we come to know You more clearly, love You more dearly and follow You more nearly, day by day. Amen.

PREFACE

"You have made known to me the path of life; you will fill me with joy in your presence, with eternal pleasures at your right hand." Psalm 16:11

Traveling off-road is never easy. It has unexpected bumps and deep potholes one would not have to endure if driving on a smooth four lane highway, lined with side-guards and neat white paint dotted down the middle. But the expected route, our route, is not always where God wants to take us. Rather, life may be a set of detours. We think we have it all figured out, and then another obstacle barricades our path.

As I fly from Ft. Dalphin, Madagascar, to Toliara, I observe a mishmash of dirt roads and attempted infrastructure. From 20,000 feet, I peek through clouds and my eyes follow a dirt trail winding its way through the spiny forest only to suddenly stop, many times at a river. I notice the road continues on the other side, There's no way around the river – one must cross it – either by a "floating bridge" or fording the river in a 4x4, hoping not to get stuck in the middle.

Such is the road of life. Eagerly we travel and anticipate the arrival at our destination, only to find an obstacle along the path. Can we learn to enjoy the journey rather than solely anticipate our arrival and destination? Can we trust?

Many times we fear the unexpected detour. Where will it take us? Where does it lead? We resist. We question. We fight the system. We would rather stay with the ordinary status quo and travel the safe, easy path knowing the road in front of us. But life doesn't always dish us soft-serve ice-cream. Sometimes it gives us green vegetables knowing spinach is better for us in the long run. Whatever our scoop of life, may God help us to savor it.

One evening a while back, we had a missionary fellowship meeting at an Australian friend's house. I was observing the conversation between father and son.

With excitement drawn from visitors, the son exclaimed, "I am going to play inside and then…I am going to play hide and seek and then… I am going to read some books…and then play with my truck…

"And first, you are going to bed, my son."

That loving conversation of a father's guiding love reminds me of Proverbs 16:9, "In his heart a man plans his course, but the LORD determines his steps."

Have you ever had your mind made up, just to experience an unexpected detour? Has the road of life taken you on an off-road safari? Maybe you, like me, will find solace in the following prayer when you are caught in the detour.

"My Lord God, I have no idea where I am going. I do not see the road ahead of me. I cannot know for certain where it will end. Nor do I really know myself, and the fact that I think I am following your will does not mean that I am actually doing so. But I believe that the desire to please you does in fact please you. And I hope that I have that desire in all that I am doing. I hope that I will never do anything apart from that desire. And I know that if I do this you will lead me by the right road, though I may know nothing about it. Therefore, I will trust you always though I may seem to be lost and in the shadow of death. I will not fear, for you are ever with me, and you will never leave me to face my perils alone."

Thomas Merton, *Thoughts in Solitude*

CHAPTER ONE

THE DETOUR

"Don't let your worries get the best of you. Remember Moses started out as a basket case."

It wasn't my intent that only five days after arriving in Africa, and just recovering from jet-lag, that I would be spending so many hours with the Tigoni police! Although much shorter than our usual flights to Madagascar, the trip to Kenya was a long one. Flying non-stop from Montreal, Canada, we had a 15 hour lay-over in London, and were thankfully met by dear friends who hosted Corbi, Charese and me for a lovely day in London.

Only five nights later, in the early morning hours of Saturday, January 11th, 2003, my first night of engaging in my new role as manager of St. Julian's Centre, the main house was robbed. It appeared to be an inside job. I spent the next several days not only as the new manager, but also as private investigator, defense attorney and judge. If I learned anything during my first ten days in Kenya, it was that there were some knowledgeable and fine Tigoni policemen. However, unless they were pushed to continue the investigation, time would slip by and the culprit would go free.

I was involved in presenting the case to the police and gathering evidence at the scene. Much like the game of CLUE®, I had to evaluate the suspects and the evidence to draw conclusions about the theft. The only difference in this case was that it was not a board game with plastic pieces representing Miss Scarlet in the library with the wrench! No, this was the game of life – making it all the more important that the evidence be clear and concise. Like Nancy Drew in a mystery novel, I had to organize data and question all eighteen staff members at St. Julian's. I even drove three hours (across the equator!) to question a suspect. There were no broken windows, causing the police and me to conclude that this was an inside job.

When the break-in was discovered by the kitchen staff and receptionist at 7:00 a.m., I was immediately summoned. With toothbrush in hand, I walked from the bathroom sink and picked up the bedside telephone.

"Hello."

"Mama (as they call their respected female elders), there is something wrong here. It seems to be very serious. I think you should come."

"I will be right there."

Hastily brushing my teeth and clipping my still wet hair, I left the manager's house and went through the back door of the main house, next to the kitchen.

"There has been a robbery," a staff member explained. "Many things have been stolen."

Taking a deep breath, I inwardly encouraged myself. *Don't panic.* "Show me what has happened," I asked the staff workers.

"Linens have been taken from the dining hall and the rugs and TV are gone!"

"We need to take an inventory," I explained. Unlocking my office door to get a clipboard and pen, I thankfully expressed gratitude to God as both computers and the cash box were in place. The 'thieves' had left the locked office untouched.

"Susan, we need to go room to room and write down what is missing. Security, call the police. Staff, please don't touch anything. Housekeeping, don't dust or sweep in the areas intruded by the thieves. Kitchen and dining hall staff, go about work as usual. We must get busy! We have 32 guests coming in less than two hours!"

With clipboard in hand, we assessed the damage to the library. The rug was removed, but the furniture had been returned to the normal positions. The phone was unplugged and stolen. And what I next noticed missing almost made me giggle. Missing were the *U.S. News and World Report* magazines, over eight months old. *Why would a professional thief steal magazines?*

We continued to the lounge. On the way, in the hallway, I noticed three pictures missing; all painted by the first manager and renovator of St. Julian's, Barbara Lutton. One picture was missing by the office door, one by the reception side door and one in the hallway leading to the lounges. *Why is there such a random selection of stolen paintings? Why didn't the thief take the whole line of paintings displayed on the wall?* These cunning intruders seemed to be picky about their selections. Recording the facts on my clipboard, I walked into the lounge.

"The TV and VCR are missing!" exclaimed a staff member.

"They took the beautiful navy blue rug," I said.

It is interesting to note what is particular to people. TV's and VCR's have never been significant to me. I tend not to watch TV. The VCR cassettes and a second rug were reported missing. These thieves took their time. They removed rugs and replaced the furniture. They had thoughtfully selected specific paintings. They took the blue-colored candy dish and matching vase. They also took the curio set of three pheasants placed on the mantle between the fireplace and piano. *Why would a group of thugs want a curio set and fragile items with no re-sale value?* I again noted the information on my clipboard.

In the lounge, we found the place of exit – the large sliding glass door leading out to the back yard and over to the back gate.

"Finger prints!" I warned the staff. "Please, do not touch. In this room lies important evidence. If you touch anything, you may also be accused."

Quickly, the staff left, not wanting to leave a trace of themselves behind. We closed the door and roped the area, making a sign reading, "Please do not enter." With 32 guests coming in less than an hour, it would be a challenge to keep the evidence undisturbed.

As soon as I walked into the dining hall, I noticed something particularly bizarre…five soda bottles had been drunk and replaced with caps back on – back in order, Coke, Fanta, Coke, Fanta, Coke. The sixth bottle went untouched. *The thieves don't like soda water,* I concluded.

The linens from two tables had been removed, and the small centerpiece had been returned to the middle of the table. The linen closet was empty – causing us to use white bed sheets from housekeeping and scrap materials found in the manager's house to prepare the tables for the day's visitors.

"The radio cassette player and tapes are missing," panicked a staff member. *And two more of Barbara Luttton's paintings,* I thought as I wrote the detailed findings in the dining hall.

*****

CSI AFRICA

At 7:20 a.m. the Tigoni Police were called by our head guard and I received hands-on training on how to use the security system. With one button in the main house and two in the manager's, a person pushes the red button, and turns the key, thus causing a silent alarm alerting Securicor, our security company.

Within five minutes, sirens were blaring and the blue Securicor truck bumped off the dirt road into the grounds of St. Julian's. Three large men (wearing helmets and face guards like American football players, covered with winter caps reminded me more of the Grinch who stole Christmas than policemen), hurriedly exited their automobile and saluted me like a sergeant would an army commander. *"There was no time for a handshake,"* the alert guard explained later.

When the three men saw me waiving hello with a clipboard in hand, they relaxed and realized there was no longer an intruder on the grounds. After congenial introductions, we entered the hacienda style main house, walking from room to room, looking over the remaining evidence left by novice burglars. Like an actress in CSI, I played a new part of the movie of life as I continued to ponder why the thieves took such a conglomeration of articles.

It wasn't much longer before the Tigoni Police came. Like Sherlock Holmes and Watson, we teamed up to draw conclusions. "Definitely, this was an inside job," said the tall, husky African police officer. People came out of the wood-work – a private investigator, police personnel, but not until four days later did the special crime scene services come for fingerprints.

The investigation was a long and drawn out process. But one fact was sure. My God, the God of the Universe was with me each step of the way. Proverbs 2:1-7 became very real to me during that time of challenge in Kenya. *"My son (and daughter), if you accept my words and store up my commands within you, turning your ear to wisdom and applying your heart to understanding, and if you cry out for insight and cry aloud for understanding, and if you look for it as for silver and search for it as for hidden treasure, then you will under-stand the fear of the Lord and find the knowledge of God. For the Lord gives wisdom and from His mouth comes knowledge and understanding. He holds victory in store for the upright; he is a shield for those whose walk is blameless, for he guards the course of the just and protects the way of his faithful ones."*

*****

ONE NIGHT IN THE TIGONI PRISON

I wasn't satisfied with the answers from some of the employees, so I fired three and apprehended two, detaining them in prison overnight. From the start they knew they had a no-nonsense manager. The dilapidated police station was a shock to the western eye.

Rusty old bicycles lay piled in a corner, various parts in disarray. A handwritten sign hung on the scrappy wall: "A mistake is not a crime."

Prisoners take one shoe off while in prison to discourage escape. They don't leave both shoes at the door because a pair would likely be stolen. The policeman guarding the door was wearing army boots with no shoelaces. If he ran to catch an escaped prisoner I thought he might fall out of his shoes like Cinderella.

There were two toilets for 50 prisoners living in a space no larger than a 20-foot cell. The space was so overcrowded that two people had crammed into the toilet area, standing up for 12 hours at a time. People even used toilets while they were standing right next to it.

Prisoners stole money and cigarettes from one another's pockets. At 4:35 p.m. they received their only meal for 24 hours, ugali (cornmeal) and sukomawiki (greens). The next morning they received a cup of tea

In the office where I was escorted to file statements, I noticed a half-century old typewriter dating back to 1950. Just as antique were the wooden trunks and tables. Papers were stacked in construction paper used as file folders. In this 21st Century police station, no computers, no TV, no file cabinets, no telephone.

Besides the broken down bicycles, the courtyard contained a pile of old tires, dirty orange buckets and rusted barbed wire. Old trucks, remained stationary for years, and I wondered if the rusty BMW would even start up. Rocks held down plastic on the building's leaky roof. Tangled electrical lines hung in disarray like cooked spaghetti. Ladies' singing voices could be heard at high decibels through broken windows. The cement floor called for a coat of paint and a single light bulb was the only proof that the electrical wires were in working order.

*****

PEOPLE HAVE TEETH!

After waiting at the Tigoni prison and having a brief discussion in the car used as a makeshift office, Alex, the driver for St. Julian's Center, the Tigoni police and I decided it would be a good idea to take a road trip and go search for a former street boy who often stayed, free of charge, at St. Julian's. Was he really at boarding school like he told us on Monday morning when he left his belongings at St. Julian's? Or was he part of the group of thieves? Time would tell, and at this moment, time consisted of a three-hour road trip to Mt. Kenya.

While waiting for the armed police to gather a few belongings and escort us on the northern road towards the equator, I scribbled a list on my hand. *What do I grab for this unique road trip?* Map, water, pillow, purse, ID, International Driver's license, toilet paper, hat and sunscreen (I would be on the left side of the vehicle, driving north with no air conditioning in mid-summer on the equator) and Kiswahili language book. I am the minority in the car. Their mother tongue is Kiswahili and they spoke it all the way.

I now understood my past 11 years of missionary service in Madagascar was just training ground for my new mission in Kenya.

This time last week the girls and I were squashed in the normally five passenger mini-station wagon with our preciously packed possessions from the USA: 2 plastic trunks, 4 suitcases, 3 carry-on suitcases, 3 purses, 1 autoharp; 1 camcorder, 1 35 mm camera. How did we squeeze it all in?

Glancing out the window, I observed my new surroundings. A single man was transporting three bamboo chairs on a bicycle. I decided that Kenya was much like Madagascar. Broken down cars were abandoned on the side of the road. Pick-up trucks were overloaded with various paraphernalia three times their size, and it was not unusual to see two or even three people on a bicycle sometimes carrying a *gony* (sack) of charcoal! Ten people would gather to watch a single man change a tire.

Roadside fruit stands dotted the road, reminding me that my girls loved stopping to purchase local sugar cane. Entrepreneurs gathered sand from the local river, piling it roadside, hoping to make a day's wages of approximately two or three dollars a day, double that of Madagascar but still so minimal it would only buy a large pack of gum in the USA. People also carried chickens by their feet, and we passed one of the few (if only) hydroelectric plants in the country. The local fisherman had caught fresh fish, which were still hanging on the line. He extended his hand hoping for a sale.

I observed ways in which Kenya was a bit more sophisticated than Madagascar: they tie the sack at the top of the charcoal so it doesn't fall out; railways seem to work; they have at least one 4-lane divided highway, called a British carriage. Like Madagascar, people transport goods on their heads, but here are Thika trees, not Baobab, and lovely houses dot the countryside. In Kenya there are overpasses, in Madagascar it was a single road for 1,000 miles. And there are street signs, in English! Roadside fruit stands line the road, but the apples are wrapped in plastic, not sold in a raffia basket. I was amazed at the pineapple plantations and later found out that it was the Dole Food Company, Inc.

The grass on the roadside was cut with a mower, not a single pair of hedge scissors. There were yield signs and Kenol service stations with small shops selling drinks and snacks. Matatu's, the local mini-vans transporting were driven fast, too fast in my opinion, and electrical lines outside the city seemed to give 24 hour service. Huts were made of timber and clay. Donkeys, zebra, goats and cattle could be counted for roadside scrimmage. Much to my amazement were the grocery stores - even in the more rural towns! And the trees! Yes, there were trees! There was not the slashing and burning found in Madagascar. Most astounding to me was that in Kenya, people have teeth, carry umbrellas, and wear shoes - things the local Malagasy considered luxury.

We arrived at the school and during the three-hour interview with the teenage boy, God was impressing upon my heart that something did not add up. Even though there was no concrete evidence I was putting the picture together. I could not prove he was involved, however, as the manager of St. Julian's Centre I exercised my authority and asked him not to come back to the Centre. With police at my side, I knew that this would be enforced at all levels.

He had teamed up with other staff members; and so after I fired three and put two in jail, the rest of the staff knew I was boss. We had no more major theft incidents for the rest of my time at St. Julian's Centre.

*****

JURY DUTY

I had been called for jury duty in Florida on January 3rd but had to turn it down, as I would be out of the country. Little did I know at that time that I was to be the real juror (and judge) a few weeks later – in Africa.

Movie star Rachel Weisz states in an article for *British Airlines High Life Magazine*, "You can't prepare for Kenya. Filming *The Constant Gardener* was a more emotional experience – one of the most extraordinary life-changing things I've ever done." I would have to agree with her. Although I felt that Madagascar had somewhat prepared me for my new role as Manager of St.

Julian's Centre, nothing could have really prepared me for this off-road safari.

I needed to get off this treadmill of playing detective. I had to move on. In my western thinking, I needed to find the culprit of the robbery. It seems in western culture, everything must have a conclusion – all the ends tied – all the ducks in a row – otherwise things remain unraveled, incomplete, perhaps even somewhat confused. But obtaining a just conclusion wasn't going to happen this time. I was no longer in my western world, but in a completely different African culture. Did it really matter that the culprit was locked up or was it more important that now, through solid investigation, I could trust my staff at St. Julian's Centre? I learned the importance of the latter. The robbers were never found, but I gained confidence to persevere in the journey and use the gifts given by God for the appointed time.

Life is what you make it. We can choose: suffer through the detour or enjoy the journey.

LESSONS LEARNED ALONG THE DETOUR:

This robbery forced me to grow in confidence and use the gifts God gave me for the appointed time. As I depended upon Christ and Christ alone, He used the detour to equip me to move ahead on the path and accomplish even more than I could ever ask or imagine.

DETOUR PRAYER:

Lord Jesus, as we journey along the road of life and some-times take an alternative route, may we endure the bumps and potholes of an off-road safari with grace. Help us to always remember that even though we think we have our way mapped out and put into our GPS, Your ways are not always our ways and Your will is not always our will. Help us always to remember: "In his heart a man plans his course, the LORD determines his steps." (Proverbs 16:9)

CHAPTER TWO

WHAT TO DO WHEN YOU DON'T KNOW WHERE YOU ARE GOING

If God is your co-pilot, swap seats.

Tension mounts when it comes to road trips. Many marital squabbles seem to revolve around what to do when you don't know where you are going. My first instinct is to stop and ask directions. My husband's is to try and figure it out on his own. Sometimes our squabbles are lessened by the GPS my sister and brother-in-law bought for us one Christmas. However, if just one number is off, the GPS can lead to a totally different destination, making us even further off-course. If we take a route different than the one given by the GPS, the voice repeats, "recalculating!" until we are back on the path.

Whatever the method, we seem to always get to our final ending point, although sometimes much later than expected. Sometimes we take what we now call, the "scenic route."

Sometimes faith follows a similar path. We are not sure where we are going. Fog covers the road or a detour causes confusion in the journey ahead. We are blinded by the storm, unsure of the road ahead. Scared. Sightless. Perhaps even spiritually paralyzed. But in reality, "faith is believing in advance what only makes sense in reverse". (Hebrews 11:1)

Faith is many times more than a mental exercise – it is an action. For me, faith has to have wheels on. By faith, we have to put into action what we believe we have heard from God.

Several months prior to leaving Madagascar, we weren't even considering a move from the Red Island. On my 42nd birthday, Monday, August 21, 2001, I woke up in the middle of the night and wrote the following dream in my journal.

"Jane Butterfield, Titus Pressler, Todd and myself are together with other missionaries. It is reunion time. I am not sure where we are, but it is someone else's country.

After getting pizza, we drive up to the hotel. The girls are not with us. As we drive up, we notice a detour. In the hotel parking lot the military police demand that we board another bus. Where are we going? I struggle. I do not even have my purse, or any forms of identity, because I had just gone to get pizza with my husband! If they find out I have boarded the bus without identity, they can arrest and imprison me.

Quickly I leave the group for just a few minutes to go to the first floor and pick up my purse in the hotel room. The military officer turns his head and pretends not to notice that I have left the group.

Nathalie is holding the elevator button open for me. Arrow up! "Go quickly, girlfriend," she says to me. Will they notice I am gone? Thank God the first floor is not far. I grab my purse. Corbi's "huggy bear" is there. Do I grab that too and risk them noticing that I have extra baggage? Leave the black duffel. Grab your purse. Run to the elevator… Quickly…quickly….quickly….

It took me a few months to begin to understand this dream and over time I interpreted it as a sign from God that we would be leaving Madagascar sooner than we had planned. While Todd took a two week jaunt out to the rainforest to build a health clinic, (walking over 100 miles on foot!), I had the urge to pack. As a squirrel storing nuts for the winter, I was getting prepared. As I did not want to startle the girls, I packed during the midnight hours. I wanted to keep life as normal as possible. Packing a suitcase might cause the girls concern. However, when picture frames started coming off the walls, I knew I had to tell them.

After revealing my dream to them one morning over breakfast on the balcony, I had their full support. *"That makes so much sense, Mom!"* said Charese.

"It does?" I questioned.

"Yes! Do you remember the dream I had about six months ago? The one about the soldier running after us? Dad and Corbi became separated

from us. You and I were together. The men were running after us, shouting, 'No redheads allowed in the city!"

Time did not allow much discussion that morning, for our ride was coming to take us to school. But time went on, and the girls and I were mentally prepared if something was going to happen.

I told my bishop that we might be leaving. Archbishop Remi was flying out to the rainforest on the helicopter that was to pick up Todd. Before he even greeted my husband, he implored him to *'speak with your wife.'* In his eyes, I was talking nonsense, something about leaving.

Time continued to pass and no move seemed imminent. Few people around me understood.

Todd will admit that he didn't have the same point of view as I about the possibility of our leaving. Therefore, we had a deal. If nothing happened by January, I would unpack our suit-cases. January arrived and there were still no signs of moving, but I still refused to unpack my suitcase. Still holding true to my conviction I that I heard from God, my packed suitcase was my symbol of faith, my umbrella. When we pray for rain, faith means that we carry an umbrella. I had asked God to speak to me, and my packed suitcase was my umbrella.

The only mystery was the timing.

*****

16 PEOPLE TO TELL WHAT TO DO

A few months after the dream, we were contacted by Rift Valley Academy (RVA) and told that our children's names were now first and second on the waiting list, which they had been on for five years. Most likely, places would become available for our children to attend their school in the near future.

We took a quick trip to Kenya in January 2002 to visit the school. While there, the political situation in Madagascar began to heat up and Air Madagascar closed down, forcing us to stay in Kenya for an extra week. During that time our family had a wonderful time staying at St. Julian's Centre and being close to the Village Market. With bowling, movies, putt-putt golf and a small water park we were happily entertained.

The missionaries who were renovating St. Julian's Centre came and said they needed to go back to the USA earlier than planned for medical reasons and would we be the new managers to get it up and running again? Todd quickly passed it off to me.

"*Patsy can do that,*" he stated.

"*Me? How can I do that? I have not any business experience. I am a Health and PE teacher.*"

"*Well, you have been telling me what to do for 18 years*", reasoned Todd. *"You will be in your element. You will have 16 people to tell what to do."*

16 people to tell what to do? Humm, I thought to myself, sure, I might like that job.

Why does the Father make us wait for periods of time for the answer? Waiting on God develops intimacy. Although we knew we were going to move to Kenya for the girls to attend school at Rift Valley Academy, the validity of my dream was borne out as the political situation in Madagascar heated up.

In May of 2002 we left Madagascar, The U.S. government personnel had advised all non-essential personnel to leave the island months before. Companies demanded that employees evacuate. The expected route had come to an end, and a detour stood before us. We left Madagascar earlier than anticipated, beginning a new chapter of life in Kenya.

*****

TEARS OF FRIENDSHIP CAN NEVER BE WIPED AWAY

In the summer of 2002, Todd expressed his sentiments in a newsletter written to family, friends and supporters. He wrote:

"Breaking Up is Hard to Do. These words are lyrics to a popular hit song in the 1970's. Recently, I have found myself singing them over and over again, one generation later.

Everyone from time to time struggles with breaking up. The Malagasy people have been in turmoil since their election results started coming in at the end of December 2001.

Somehow, the election results reported by the government (and supported by the incumbent President) had not been the same as the results reported by the observers sent to represent the people. The Malagasy people living in the capital had gone to the streets and protested the fraudulent results.

Over the course of the last five months, the political situation in Madagascar had deteriorated. Presently in Madagascar there were two Presidents, the incumbent leader and a new leader elected by the people. There seemed to be two of everything: two governments, two capitals, and two presidents. Change is demanding. Breaking up is hard to do.

Fighting had been reported in three of the provinces, mostly led by the former President, who refused to step down. He had induced ethnic discrimination and enticed people to fight against each other. Over 60 people had been killed as a result and he had blocked or blown up numerous bridges and roads leading to Antananarivo, the original capital. Since the end of February when these acts of destruction had begun, the capital had been without fuel, flour, sugar, salt, oil and other consumables. Major textile companies have temporarily closed or permanently left Madagascar because they are not able to import or export materials caused by the roadblocks. The United Nations reported last week that 65,000 people had lost their jobs and the economy was losing between 12-14 million dollars a day. Imagine what this had done to the economy of the 11th poorest country in the world! The former President did not want to break up his government, his economic wealth, his ties to corruption, his ties to France, nor his ties to international prestige.

Breaking up is hard to do. In the midst of this political situation we had been contemplating our future missionary role. For some time, we had known that Corbi and Charese would be going away to boarding school. Five years ago we had applied to Rift Valley Academy (RVA) in Kenya, anticipating the day when they would need to attend a larger school providing broader sports competition, social interaction, and numerous electives in a Christian environment. After visiting RVA in February of this year, it had become very evident that it was going to be hard for us to be separated from our children. So, we decided to move to Kenya to be closer to them. As a matter of fact, we would be only thirty-five minutes away.

Beginning in January 2003, Patsy will become the Director/Manager of St. Julian's Centre (conference and retreat centre), which is being renovated by Episcopal missionaries. I will be a "non-resident" missionary serving in three provinces, Kenya, Madagascar and Sudan and will assist Patsy at St. Julian's.

Our last two weeks in Madagascar had been very difficult and emotional days for our family. Having to say "goodbye" to Archbishop Remi Rabenirina, to our Malagasy colleagues, to our Malagasy missionary and expatriate friends and to our staff had been very difficult. The day before we left, we had the dedication of the Lay Training Centre. As it came time for me to speak, my eyes welled up with tears, my heart started pounding and my voice cracked as I stated how difficult it was "to break up." I shared with the people that what makes it so difficult to say goodbye or "until later" was not the ministry that we had together (the building of nine dispensaries, the lay training centre or the several churches), but rather the friendships that we had nurtured. We had traveled into the rain forest, spent time in fellowship, performed weddings, wept through funerals, celebrated anniversaries, endured graduations, visited the sick, attended confirmations and baptisms, shared meals and broken bread together at the Lord's Table. This place had been our home and we had shared our lives together. I was thankful to my Malagasy friends who had made me a more complete person, a godlier person. It was not so much what I had contributed to them, but rather what they had shared with me. That is what makes breaking up hard to do.

I think it is appropriate to end with a well-known Bible passage from Ecclesiastes. "There is a time for everything, and a season for every activity under heaven…A time to plant and time to uproot…A time to tear down and time to build…A time to weep and time to laugh…"

As I look back and compare the day we arrived in Madagascar, August 2nd, 1991, with the day we left May 14th, 2002, I see how our loyal Malagasy friends had always been present. They had been there to meet us and send us off in large numbers. They had assisted us with our luggage and greeted us with love. We had laughed together when they mentioned that upon our arrival they were looking for someone who looked like MacGyver. At our departure, they had stood silently when we said goodbye. Quietly, we had wept together. The most moving experience was at the airport when Archbishop Remi, who is not known to frequently share his emotions, said goodbye, hugged us and began to cry. He never wiped away his tears as they welled up in his eyes and dribbled down his brown, plump cheeks. As I reflect on this moment, I have an inspirational thought: Tears of friendship can never be wiped away."

*****

FROM THE GIRLS' POINT OF VIEW

"We have left from the terrible tragedies that have happened in Madagascar but now we are safe in a sweet, silent place in Kenya, called St. Julian's. The staff's loving kindness has made us feel more at home. But the staff knows that Madagascar was home and encouraged us to stand strong in the love of Jesus.

The transition will be hard to move from a home to a place I barely know. But I trust God will help us in the transition. In God's name we trust." —Corbi

"It is beautiful. The scenery is gorgeous. The staff is so kind to us. Every day we work either in the gardens or in the kitchen. I like working in the kitchen better because I like cooking and the staff are very friendly. I miss my best friend in

Madagascar but the staff has been friendly to me. Mom made up this prayer walk. I like to take this walk because the birds are pretty and they sing beautifully. When we come to live here we will have three cats. Their names are Bernadette, Socks and Mister. We will have dogs, too. Their names are Square, Tom and the puppies are Joan and Lou. So when we come back next year, I am happy we will have animals. Oh, I forgot. We have a donkey too! Cool!" —Charese

*****

RVA – NOT A BAD PLACE TO BE!

The girls adjusted to life in Kenya and boarding school without too many hitches. Expressing themselves in a newsletter a few months later they described life on the African mainland as an exciting adventure.

"RVA (Rift Valley Academy) is really a blast! I have made several friends, especially those girls who live in my dorm. My roommates are Priscilla and Jin-Sal who are from South Korea. Their parents are missionaries. Priscilla's parents are in Yemen and she has been at RVA for three years. Jin-Sal was new last August and her parents are in Dar Salaam, Tanzania. I like almost everything about RVA, so it's hard for me to pick one favorite thing. But, I guess I would say my friends and the other people on campus because everybody is friendly, smiles and says 'hello'. My dorm parents are really cool and sweet like sugar. They understand a lot of stuff that's happening in my life, like my transition and the theft at St. Julian's. If I ever get worried or scared, I always ask them to pray for me and my mom, and sometimes we pray together." — Charese

"The Rift Valley Academy campus is located on a mountainside where students can look down and see the beautiful view overlooking the lower Rift Valley. Sunsets are beautiful and two nights ago I saw a full moon rise when friends and I were playing soccer until it was so dark we couldn't even see the ball in front of us. I am playing the flute in band and playing soccer. My extracurricular class is art, taught by a very cool male teacher. My 8th grade girls' dorm is in the middle of campus so I don't have to walk too far to any of my classes. My roommates are Sarah, Chris and Esther. Esther is Kenyan, Sarah and Chris are American missionary children living in Africa. Linda, another friend of mine, has a father who is a carpenter and a mother who works in the financial department for their mission. Her parents live twelve hours away from RVA. I am so thankful that my parents only live 35 minutes away! My mom tries to come to RVA once a week and some weekends we get to go home. Although I am still going through a somewhat difficult transition, RVA is not a bad place to be!" Corbi, Spring 2003

LESSONS LEARNED ALONG THE DETOUR:

What do you do when you don't know where you are going? If you are like me, you might tend to panic and an unsettling feeling comes into the pit of your stomach. Irritability might be at hand. I remember the advice Elisabeth Elliot gave me as she reflected upon the death of her first husband who was killed by the Auca Indians in Ecuador. "Do the next thing." When we are not sure of the path ahead, just do the next thing. Trust God.

DETOUR PRAYER:

Lord, help me remember that You are always with me along my journey in life. Even when I don't know where I am going or what I am doing – when the fog is thick and clouds hem me in – help me to trust You for the next step and just do the next thing. Maybe then I can begin to pray, "Show me Your ways, O Lord, teach me Your paths, Guide me in Your truth and teach me, for You are God my Savior, and my hope is in you all day long." (Ps. 25:4-5)

CHAPTER THREE

AN OFF-ROAD SAFARI

*The good Lord didn't create anything without a purpose,
but mosquitoes and sand gnats come close.*

I saw the guns first. Five men followed.
"Everybody! Down on the floor!"

It was a peaceful Sunday afternoon, until the hostile attack. After a lovely Kenyan meal of chapatti, *ugali* (corn meal) and *nyama choma* (grilled goat) at a St. Paul's professor's home, several of us chatted in their living room drinking local chai. Charese was seated next to Todd and me on the couch to my left, only a few people away. Several other professors and co-workers from St. Paul's United Theological College joined in conversation about international and theological issues.

The thugs must have seen cars parked in the driveway and decided to take advantage of the situation. After a loud knock on the door, a man asked for the owner of the house. When the owner went to the door, the man barged in, pulled out a pistol hidden under his clothing and pushed the owner on the ground. Four more men with AK 47's and machine guns barged in. Speaking Kiswahili, they demanded jewelry, money and phones. Face down on the ground, Todd handed to the robber his heirloom wedding band passed down from Grandfather Cox while I hid mine under a pillow. Todd gave his wallet and personal money, I gave my watch and a few hundred dollars of money just received from selling my first book, *A Guest in God's World: Memories of Madagascar.*

Quick thinking Todd began to negotiate. He asked for the robbers to return his credit cards and ID information which would be no use to them. They eventually granted his request, throwing it on the ground. When the Dr. lying on the ground next to Todd could not get his wedding band off instantly, one of the thugs hit him with the butt of an AK 47, causing him to bleed slightly. The other men completed full searches on the women, as we lay helplessly on the ground. After 7-9 minutes, they finally left, leaving everybody shaken and scared. Trusting in God, we prayed as a group to the Lord.

Life does not come without challenges. We can't always choose the road nor the circumstance the detour might bring. But perseverance produces character and the attack we endured on Palm Sunday in April 2004 was no exception.

The letters we received from friends through email brought much healing and comfort.

"Dearest Patsy, Todd and Charese,

"Please know that we are lifting you up in our prayers and that we also did so with many others at the Chapel yesterday morning. We thank God for your preservation and know His graciousness and his mighty hand protected you. Todd, we are so sorry to learn that your wedding ring was taken and I pray that by some miraculous act its holy symbolism will be restored to you in a new way. Please know that you are all in our prayers constantly. Charese, you have gone through so much! We are so grateful to hear that you have sought and found comfort, solace and direction in the wisdom of God's Word. You are an amazing young lady and we are privileged to know you. Patsy, I can only think as a mother how horrific this experience must have been for you. I pray for an extra dose of the healing power of the Holy Spirit. We love you all and are so grateful that we can pray on your behalf. May the Lord place a hedge of protection around you and may no evil find you. God bless. Love, Christina, Doug and Nick"

"Charese, your depth in spirituality and your witness to this is so beyond your years. After your beautifully written email, I was called to read Mark 10:14-15 'When Jesus saw this, he was indignant. He said to them, 'Let the little children come to me, and do not hinder them, for the kingdom of God belongs to such as these. I tell you the truth, anyone who will not receive the kingdom of God like a little child will never enter it.'' Thank you for sharing the scriptures with me, especially Matthew 5. Many of us judge others and hold anger that really does lock our hearts and our spirits. That is not what God wants for sure. Also, Philippians, really all of Chapter 2, in being like Christ is something I need to read

daily to be reminded in my thoughts and action. I am going to keep your email in my Bible referring to it daily in my devotions.

"I remember something I recently read, actually it is in the book I sent your mom, 'Having a Mary's Heart in a Martha's World', and many times God tests us so we can give a TESTimony. You are certainly doing that. She also writes about taking a worry and turning into prayer. You again are doing that.

"I will continue to pray for you, turning my worry into a prayer. You, my dear, are something else. I only wish I could put my arms around you. Love, Cheryl"

Don't you admire others when trials and tribulations don't inhibit them from doing the will of God? The fear of this robbery did not prevent short-term missionaries from coming to partake in the Great Commission. Among others, Will, Cheryl, Christian, Doug and Nick were all on the first People Reaching People mission trip coming to Kenya just two months later. During this detour of life, people prayed for "the grace to forgive, the strength to go on and His peace that passes understanding for each day and night!" Thank you, dear body of Christ!

*****

We all have a story and we all have detours on the road of life. Will we allow these detours to inhibit us from doing the will of God, or will we allow God to work through the unexpected in our lives?

SCORPION BITE!
By the Rev. Todd McGregor

My finger throbbed in excruciating pain and a plastic bag functioned as a tourniquet. The northern Kenya medical treatment for a scorpion bite consisted of gasoline and some type of traditional ointment that my students had just applied to the infected area. Just minutes earlier I had been checking to make sure I had enough film in my camera for the upcoming baptismal service – our first in this new village. I knew it was going to be a long service as over 400 came to faith in Christ over the past few days and approximately 200 had decided to be baptized on that Sunday morning. In that camera case also awaited a sleeping scorpion, until I disturbed it.

Immediately after calling my group and informing them of the scorpion sting, I had five students by my side. One removed the scorpion from the camera case and crushed it on the ground with a pointed stick.

"*What are we going to do now?*" one evangelist asked, aware that the last person bit by a scorpion in the area was very sick and out of commission for two days.

"*We are going to have a baptismal service – starting in 30 minutes!*" I responded. After a short prayer for healing, that is exactly what we did and I remained strong for the five-hour service and baptisms for 200 Samburu new Christians.

The Lord was gracious to us as we arrived at Kamboe, 40 km south of Marsabit. On the previous Tuesday a team of thirty people had been invited to come and begin our primary evangelism mission among the beautifully beaded Samburu people. Every morning we sent out five groups into each village (*manyatta*) to share the creation and redemption story. In the hot afternoons, some of our men would gather under the sacred acacia tree with the elders of the community while our women would gather with the ladies and children under other trees. In the Samburu culture (cousins to the Maasai), there are certain places which women and men are forbidden to gather together in public.

After the brilliant sunset, we would gather people and teach new songs, share from the Word of God, and watch *The Jesus Film*. Not until the Samburu people left would we eat and head to bed on a thin mattress, sleeping under the stars in the open canvas tent.

I was exhausted from the six-day evangelism mission. Using the wordless book, *The Evangelcube and the Four Spiritual Laws*, we taught the Samburu, who believed in African Traditional Religion, how to have faith in Christ. Focusing on Acts 2:42, we prepared them for their baptism. Some clergy spend their whole lifetime baptizing 200 people. Here, with this receptive group, it was done in one day. Over the past year I have had the opportunity to baptize over 500 new Christians in Northern Kenya and thousands have come to faith.

Some people ask me how we do this. "The grace of God is already moving in the lives of the people. We just come and make the connection."

*****

WAITING FOR THE CLOUD TO MOVE

The birds-eye view from the squeezed 6-seater Cessna confirmed the fact that we were on the edge of the Chelbi dessert. Not a person nor animal was in sight. Not a bush to hide behind for natural relief nor a bird to hear chirp. Nothing. Absolutely nothing. My first thoughts? It looked like Mars…a…bit.

Todd wanted to show the girls and me the area where he believed God was calling him to serve the Lord, so the four of us chartered a flight with Mission Aviation Fellowship and flew to Northern Kenya. Marsabit is a mountain in the middle of the desert. Because of the cloud cover hovering over the mountain, we were unable to land and the pilot had to divert the flight to Shegel. We were delayed there for over an hour in the hot sun until the cloud cover dissipated and we could see the mountain. When we could catch sight of the peak, the pilot knew it was safe to try and land.

While we waited for the cloud to move, it reminded me of how the Israelites in the desert depended upon God's guidance – waiting for the cloud to move. They lingered, hanging around for God to give them guidance on when to continue their journey.

Discernment of God's will can be like a thick cloud on a cool morning. Sometimes it is difficult to see the hand in front of us. Sometimes we barely feel His touch. Missionaries are not always without doubt and fears of their own. One day, as I was at my "Women at Ten" Bible study group in Kenya, I had a hard time expressing my thoughts in journal form, so I wrote a poem. It was the day before leaving for a trip to Northern Kenya with Bishop Waqo, where we met up with Todd who was already in Marsabit. Looking back, perhaps the poem was somewhat prophetic about what was to come later.

"O God, you are my God, earnestly I seek you. My soul thirsts for you, my body longs for you, in a dry and weary land where there is no water."

*****

SAFE IN HIS ARMS

I am scared, Lord
   Scared of being uncomfortable
   Scared of not having my own needs met

Scared of bandits
Scared, just scared, of the unknown

This is where I come
To gain peace within the storm
I trust these people
Therefore, I refuse to wipe my tears away

Because it's here that I come
To be open with others and myself
To be free to laugh and free to cry
To lift my journey like a sacrifice of praise
As the incense fills the room so our prayers are placed
at His feet
Spoken and unspoken requests before the Lord
All are known by Him
In His Hands we find shelter
We are safe in His arms.

I was struggling with this detour in life. Comfortable, beautiful St. Julian's Centre was a blessing for me. It was not only a place where I used my spiritual gifts, but I found out who I was – my identity - as a person, and my place in this world. Why would we want to leave it and go to the desert - back into the wilderness? Why would I want to leave the safe shelter and be vulnerable once again? Truly, I was having to consider the cost of leaving St. Julian's and go to Marsabit.

*****

OUR GOD REIGNS AND RAINS!!!
By Todd McGregor, Newsletter: Summer 2005

For the first time in three years, a cloud of water burst from the sky. Rain! Imagine anyone under three years old feeling water fall from the sky for the first time. Villages were like ghost towns. Nomadic tribes had left, packing their stick huts on top of their camels and walking for miles in search of water and better grazing area. So when we prayed for rain at the end of our two day mission, we prayed that it would be a sign from God, blessing them in their newly found faith in Jesus Christ.

A few days later, a young man came running to one of our evangelists. Eagerly, he told him that two days after our mission team left, the clouds covered over the village of Funanquibi and rain began to pour. And as if this story was not enough, God even made it more special by bringing rain ONLY to the two villages where the mission teams met. Rain did not even fall on the other side of the mountain, but just in the two small villages where the people had prayed for rain. Now drops of water come down my face when I write this story. Our God reigns!

Late in January, ten of my first year students from St. Paul's United Theological College and I traveled two days to share the good news of Christ with people from the Borana ethnic group. My students wanted to experience primary evangelism, reaching out to people who have either heard little or nothing about Christ. Considering that "unreached" people groups are less than 1% Christian, we were starting from scratch.

We spent six days with the Borana people sleeping under the stars in the semi-arid region 50 kilometers from the Kenyan/Ethiopian border. In the mornings we met in small huts conversing with those left in the village. Caring for basic needs of life, men would shepherd their sheep or cattle and search for grazing areas for the day. Women walk 13 km to collect water, search for wood used for cooking, or receive corn meal distributed by World Vision. The afternoons were a time of rest as the area is too hot for anything but sitting underneath one of the few acacia trees.

Life would pick up again in the early evening when people would gather for singing and teaching. Around 6:30 p.m. men would return, collecting their animals and milking them before coming to evening worship. Then the two villages would gather for teaching or watching the *Jesus* Film.

During our first two days, over 100 people accepted our message and came to faith in the Lord Jesus Christ. These people were so hungry for the Gospel that they would stay until after midnight to soak up the world of God. Saturday night we baptized 28 individuals, who were so touched by the services that they didn't want to go home. Finally, we needed to send them home at 12:30 a.m. because we had another service the following morning, baptizing another 27.

It was during the prayer time in our last service that the new congregation asked us to pray for rain.

"Pray for rain in a desert region."

I thought to myself. "Now that is a prayer of faith!" Hearts of faith is what these new Christians had and two days later a great cloudburst came from the sky. Praise to the living God. Our God reigns (and rains!).

*****

STOP SLEEPING BY THE FIRE

There is a story of a man who was a prisoner of war during the Korean War.

"I was in the camp for two years. The winters were the hard part. In North Korea the winters are very cold. It snows. The ground freezes. We had to sleep in drafty barracks on thin boards with one thin blanket. In winter, the guards would make charcoal fires in these barracks. They stood around the fires, warming themselves, in front of us. If you wanted to, you could take your blanket and go sleep by the fires. The guards didn't mind.

"You could always tell the prisoners who had given up hope. They would go sleep by the fire. It was warmer there. You could make it through the night without shaking from the cold. But being warmed that way lowered your resistance. The ones who slept by the fire would get sick, pneumonia or flu, or God knows what. They'd last for a while, but they wouldn't make it. They would die.

"Those of us who survived – we were the ones who never went to sleep by the fire."[i]

As Christians, we need to remember that sleeping by the fire of comfort and security might just be a short-cut to spiritual apathy and perhaps even death. Being soothed by the fire of coziness and wellbeing will lower our spiritual resistance. The blessed opportunity of joining in suffering for the Lord will cause our spiritual immune system to be strong, healthy, resisting unwanted disease. Lord, cause us to be strong and disciplined to stop resisting the detour and to take up our cross daily and follow You!

*****

DUSTY FEET

I am not sure who Eddie Asker is, but I found his poem on the back of a missionary friend's bathroom door in Madagascar. I have kept it close at hand ever since.

There's dust on your feet, Lord.
From the road you walked.
It seems almost disrespectful
Thinking of you like that

But it's true
Dirt under your fingernails
Sweat trickling down your back
As you walked the rough tracks in Galilee
Your seamless robe
Is spotless in the paintings
But life says otherwise
There must have been times
When it smelt of fish, and wood smoke

That's good, Lord.
It feels good to know
That you were part, are part, of human living.
That your words, your love
Are travel stained.
Born in turmoil of human relationships,
Nurtured in human need.
I thank you,
That salvation comes to me
In flesh and blood
Gift-wrapped in reality.

Lord help me live it
Grow my life around it, now.
Help me take the strength I need for today
From the sure knowledge
That salvation surrounds me.

There's dust on your feet, Lord.

That comforts me.

Because when I'm tired,

And vulnerable,

And hurting,

I see you look at me,

And smile.

I hear you say

"I know."

Hallelujah.

- Eddie Asker

*****

AFRICA'S CHRISTIAN SOLDIERS
By Robert Pigott
BBC Religious Affairs Correspondent, Kenya

Even a bumpy road has scenic points to enjoy. BBC flew to Africa to document the growth of the African church and our ministry in Northern Kenya. In December 2004, this documentary was aired throughout the world as an end of year wrap-up. At this time we had been in Kenya for not quite two years.

"As Christianity fights to keep its place in an increasingly secular European society, it is flourishing in parts of the developing world, particularly in Africa.

The single-engine plane wobbled violently on its approach to the dirt strip at Marsabit, but the McGregor family maintained a cheerful calm.

Two hours earlier in Nairobi the diminutive woman pilot had strapped us in and then announced: 'I'm going to pray now,' in a way that suggested more than just a perfunctory formality.

But the McGregor's – an improbably blond family of Anglican missionaries from Florida – were bouncing down safely enough amid a cloud of red dust, and about to be greeted by an impromptu committee of indigenous children posed around an ancient bicycle.

The McGregor's had arrived with the Christian message for the nomadic camel herders on Kenya's northern borders. They are what are known as the "un-reached" – people with traditional African religions never before approached by missionaries.

That task lay ahead, but today Todd and Patsy McGregor were to baptize people of the Samburu and Rendille tribes converted in previous months.

'Riot of Color'

Their distant village lay along an unpaved road, empty apart from a broken down bus and a group of baboons, which watched us reproachfully as we passed.

The baptisms took place under an acacia tree, next to a scattering of stick and cloth huts.

Todd McGregor pulled a surplice over his tropical beach shirt and used water from a stainless steel bowl to splash on the foreheads of 37 women and three men. It was a riot of color and celebration.

People dressed in orange and red, and weighed down with elaborate headdresses and multiple necklaces of beads, swayed and chanted.

The McGregor's jigged along, straw-haired daughters slapping hands with local girls.

This was not the stern Christianity of the early missionaries with their European disapproval of indigenous practices.

Instead, a new Africanized Christianity is being presented to susceptible people.

Local beliefs – including a single divine creator, a God who was once on earth and a spiritual existence after death – bear an eerie similarity to the Bible.

Modern missionaries are primed to discover such traditions, and co-opt them in the service of Christianity.

It is a softly-softly approach.

Only later will the McGregor's tackle the endemic wife-beating and female genital mutilation.

It is enough for now that women are telling us that Christianity is changing their lives, and that it is ever easier to love their husbands.

Religious Rivalry

Meanwhile, the McGregor's are pursuing their own conversion strategy.

Today it is among the un-reached people of the Gabbra tribe near the border with Ethiopia.

Unusual rains have given the arid earth of the Chalbi Desert a superficial bloom of green that is already withering in the ceaseless wind.

The family gains entry to a stick and cloth hut. They sip tea, inspect children and smile winningly.

But at a nearby settlement – where people are gathered at a well filling plastic drums with water – the atmosphere is uneasy.

Muslim missionaries have been here already.

According to the McGregors, the Muslims are even more accepting of local practices, including the unequal position of women.

The men watering camels seem indifferent to our presence, but the women are restive.

One brandishes a stone menacingly. Our local guide is getting nervous. We retreat – sparkling Floridian smiles intact – toward the Land Rover.

None of this will daunt the McGregors though.

Converting the un-reached is their purpose, their whole function. They will be back. At the outer fringe of African Christendom, the arduous battle for souls continues."

Story from BBC News:
http://news.bbc.co.uk/go/pr/fr/-/I/hi/programmes/from_our_
own_correspondent/4169273.stm
Published: 2005/01/13 10:50:30 GMT C BBC MMV

LESSONS LEARNED ALONG THE DETOUR:

All things work together for those who love God and for those who are called according to His purpose. He will use robberies…scorpion bites…challenging ministry to bring honor and glory to Him as well as bring us encouragement and strength along the journey. Everyone has a story to tell. What happened to us in the past helps to mold us into the person we are today and gives us experience for the future, no matter how difficult or pleasant, sad or happy. Our journey continues to shape and transform us, causing us to discover God in a rainbow of circumstances.

DETOUR PRAYER:

Lord, even when we wonder why You take us off-road, may we remain confident in the knowledge that in Your strong and trusty four-wheel drive, You can take us through every situation, causing it to turn out for good for those who love God and for those who are called according to His purpose. (Rom. 8:28)

CHAPTER FOUR

ON TOP OF MT. KILI!

"If you want to go far, go together.
If you want to go fast, go alone."

African Proverb

*****

ONE STEP AT A TIME
By Corbi McGregor, age 16

As I gazed up at the massive, cloud-covered mountain, doubt and anxiety filled my head. Slowly I glanced down to the picture of an elderly African man holding a child and my uncertainties vanished. Many people had flown across the oceans to join my family on this fundraising climb. Although I have lived in Africa since the age of two, climbing Mt. Kilimanjaro was something I never imagined I would do until I moved to Kenya three years ago. Before Kenya, I lived in Madagascar for 12 years where only some of our closest friends and family came to visit. Americans seemed almost scared to come to one of the poorest countries in the world. However, Kenya is different.

I glimpsed back to the picture clutched in my hand which was given to each team member as an incentive during our climb. *What beautiful people. I've learned so much from them.* The picture portrayed an unreached people group that my family works with in the isolated desert of northern Kenya. They are named the Gabbra, a nomadic group that walk their herds of camels and cattle miles at a time in search of water. Frequently my family interacts with these people, sometimes accepted with open arms and other times threatened with stones.

My thoughts drifted to one of our last visits. Surrounded by women chatting in a language I could not understand, one took my hand and we walked. Although I had never met her before, she led me along a dirt road to a small village consisting of several stick huts. It was for these people, whom we had learned to love, that we were climbing the largest free-standing mountain in the world.

Maybe it was helpful that I had not realized the difficulty of the climb. For six days we walked several hours each day at high altitudes, set up camp, ate dinner, shared stories and went to bed. Due to a lack of light, as well as a lack of strength, there wasn't much else to do, but the stories helped unite our diverse group of twenty four people, aged between 12 and 59.

Hope rose with the sun and every morning the crater at the summit of the large volcano seemed closer. But, as the climb became more difficult, the never-ending path wore us down. It was then that the strength of the group helped us to be stronger than our individual will. Walking through as many as six different terrains, from desert and rainforest jungle to the glacier ice cap, we sang and encouraged one another. The goal of the group was not only to make it to our final destination, but also to have fun along the way.

There I was at 19,000 feet – tired, dirty and watching people of all nationalities suffer from severe altitude sickness. Clutched in my frosted mitten, there was the picture that encouraged me to take one more step. The steps became miles, and eventually the entire mountain. Through heat, cold, rain and fog, at last I stood at the summit. The blue sky stretched for miles and the glistening greenish blue glacier reminded me of the sapphires found in Madagascar. This was absolutely the most beautiful place that I had ever been – and to get there, I had learned endurance, encouragement and the importance of taking just one step at a time.

*****

WEIGHING OUR PACKS

Dec. 20th 2005, 5:30 a.m.
St. Julian's Centre, Redhill, Kenya

I am up early today. Hot flashes and prayer flashes. The Florida team is flying in today and I have begun to pray for safety and rest. This trek up Mt. Kilimanjaro is a once in a lifetime – not to be rushed. I pray that even as people begin to gather that we have joy in the journey.

Phil 1:3 "I thank my God every time I remember you. In all my prayers for all of you, I always pray with joy because of your partnership in the gospel from the first day until now, being confident of this, that he who began a good work in you will carry it on to completion until the day of Christ Jesus."

This is my prayer for the mission team. These people have been with us from the beginning: Mom, Dad, Betsy, Brian, Kevin, Will, Cheryl, and the Combest-Friedman's. So many of these dear friends have persevered with us through the years. And now we are gathering all together to have a fundraising climb for the purpose of building water wells and schools for the indigenous people of Northern Kenya. Some of the group is staying back to teach VBS (Vacation Bible School) at a local church close to St. Julian's Centre. Praise be to God.

And here it is – the first day. I do ask God to carry the work that He has begun to completion. There must be so many mixed emotions. Lord, strengthen each of us for the task. Keep us humble and on our knees, knowing that each step is dependent upon You. As You have begun our journey, we ask that You would give us joy through the journey as You carry it on to completion. Praise be to the Son of God.

In choosing a journal to carry up Kilimanjaro, I asked myself, "Do I want to carry this for six days up the highest mountain in Africa? Thus, I changed from the leather bound, fancy one I received for my ordination and decided upon a small, simple, spiral notepad. The first I will save for the pulpit – and in the spiral notebook, I will squeeze every white space in the notepad and journal to the top of the mountain.

Wouldn't it be a good discipline in our own lives if we weighed our words as much as we weigh our packs to carry up Kili? As I will carry my own day pack, filled with 5 liters of drinking water, sunscreen, lip balm, sweater, and Scripture memorization cards, I am very aware of what I will need and what is to be left behind. Will what I put in my pack be beneficial or a burden?

Through life, we carry our words like trekkers carry packs up the mountain. Will what I am going to say be a benefit or a hindrance to those who listen? This reminds me of Colossians 4:6 "Let your conversation be always full of grace, seasoned with salt, so that you may know how to respond/answer everyone."

Yes, Lord. Season my words with grace. As people come to Africa for the first time, they are taken out of their comfort zone. Cause me to be sensitive to their needs. Cause me to be loving and caring and ready to serve. I need your grace to cause me to be sensitive to the needs of others. Please keep me on my knees and sensitive to You. I pray this in the Holy Name of Jesus.

*****

BWANA ASIFIWE!

Wed. Dec. 21ˢᵗ, 2005
Marsabit, Northern Kenya

The team has chartered a MAF (Mission Aviation Fellowship) flight to experience Northern Kenya before the Kilimanjaro climb to meet the people and witness the commissioning of the first six evangelists taught by Todd. They are: Samuel Shute, Daniel Huka, Elizabeth Kabale, Rose Ann Dake, Isaiah Sambuno, and Jackson Ntoke.

The new cathedral of Marsabit is just one year old. I take visual notes. The pigeons in the rafters make it difficult to hear and I notice a popped balloon tied on a string, a plastic bag lying on floor by the altar, and red and white ribbons taped to the wall, serving as Christmas decorations. The flip chart paper has fallen on floor and there is not too much fanfare for a westerner who looks at appearances. But there is no doubt! The Spirit is here! Drums beat and people sing at the top of their lungs – all with cheerful celebration and praise to the Lord! *Bwana asifiwe*! There are several choirs, a few from Sagante and one coming all the way from Sololo, a 6-hour truck ride. I notice that Jennifer and other song leaders have attached a small wooden cross to their Samburu beads worn around their necks.

Like Paul's missionary experiences and other "detours of life," God has opened and closed the door for Todd's work in Northern Kenya. Todd and Bishop Waqo were to go to Loidwar, Kacuma, Sudan. But the Lord closed the door and now has opened the door for Northern Kenya. Praise God! Bishop Waqo reminded us of that at today's commissioning service. Four months training for the evangelists – Bishop Waqo says it is like the tip of the iceberg – never stop learning! The certificates are presented. They read: Certificate of DMA Evangelism Training Institute in Marsabit ACK Kirinyaga certifies that (*Name*) has successfully completed the requirements for evangelism, Dec. 21st, 2005, in the Name of the Father, the Son and the Holy Spirit.

John 15:16 "You did not choose me, but I chose you and appointed you to go and bear fruit—fruit that will last. Then the Father will give you whatever you ask in my name." God has chosen Todd to be in Northern Kenya rather than Sudan and He has chosen each one of us for a purpose!

In the same regard, I believe God has also chosen each one of the members of this mission team. We may think that we chose to come to Africa, but actually, it is He who chose us! Cheryl and Will Harman; Mom and Dad Cox; Todd, myself,

Corbi and Charese McGregor; Betsy, Brian and Kevin Wenzel; Fay and Andrew Sommers; Arlene; Tandy Robinson; Emily; Don Wenzel; the Combest-Friedman's and their friends; Piers, Julian and Ingrid Davidson. Praise God. He has chosen each one of us!

*****

I AM BECAUSE WE ARE
John Mbiti

December 24th, 2005
St. Julian's Centre, Redhill, Kenya

It's one of our joys and habits with short-term mission teams that at the end of the day we share Christ-like Moments - moments during the day when we felt an extra presence of Christ, like a "God Incidence" or "Epiphany Moment." These Christ-like moments allow us to recapture the events of the day with the eyes of others, in another's perspective. I gain insight from sharing these moments. It allows me various sets of eyes from which to see things. Even my simple math can calculate 24 (people) x 2 (eyes each person) = 48 (eyes).

Mbiti explains it in a sentence: I am because we are. We all learn from one another and when we seek to learn from another perspective and desire to see from their viewpoint, we are then blessed to see out of 48 eyes! Its like a quilt – everybody offers their piece.

Christlike moments also allow us to see Christ in the ordinary.

Christ-like Moments:

Patsy – seeing Todd in action. Matt. 28 "I have chosen You!"

Don – children who have "nothing" have love for us.

Mom – herders in the middle of nothing, seeing bishop Waqo, who baptized them.

Betsy – all people smile in the same language, they drop everything and become hospitable.

Tandy – smile and wave is universal. Receiving us with such joy and singing. Share our joy together. Simplicity. We are all God's children; being so different (different cares, different clothing) but the same! Holding hands and looking into a woman's eyes.

Brian – trust—the children trust you immediately, they are flocking to you.

Charese – shepherd – a little boy carrying a goat on his shoulders as Jesus carried us. Especially our burdens when we are weak. Maybe that goat was the weakest.

Cheryl – "to the least of you" my thought is who is the least. The tribes especially the Samburu have such a sense of community and love and simplicity. They are so full.

Don – thankful to be part of the group. In the truck, "The Lord will protect me, right?" Thankful that he did. Thankful luggage showed up.

Faye – picking up 2 little girls – Sarah and Jacqueline. Jacqueline had a strong voice. The congregation at the first village singing in English. Meeting Pious and Rose as two ambitious students, "hope."

Will – hearing Todd's message and realizing he is doing more evangelizing than ever before by just being around Todd.

Kevin – recognizing one of my fears was that I would be so uncomfortably hot that I wouldn't like the desert – but even though Will's watch registered 90° Fahrenheit I was comfortable; coming back in the truck, banging around the pole and the kids singing took my mind off of my pain and discomfort.

Arlene – 2 little girls – Sarah and Jacqueline, got into our vans smiling and singing with trust and security not knowing us – trust in the Lord, small children with babies on their back gives them a purpose. "We all have a purpose."

Audrey – Samburu women with their beautiful garb – Rose, student in village, graduated from high school and going to college in Nairobi. Love her culture.

*****

THE GIFT OF CREATIVITY

Christmas Day (a few days before the climb) offered a time for creativity: instead of an exchange of presents, we exchanged gifts of words. Some wrote poems. Here's one from my dad who stayed back at St. Julian's Centre with a group who prayed for us and lead a Vacation Bible School for the local church.

*****

TWAS THE NIGHT BEFORE CHRISTMAS
by Gerry Cox

T'was the night before Christmas

In Kenya we know,

Desert, green hills and valleys, some water and little snow.

All quiet at St. Julian's and in their beds asleep

Was a mission team from the U.S.

Dreaming, "Praise the Lord, our souls to keep!"

Not stockings but all kinds of footwear

Were at the foot of the bed,

For this was in Kenya, what more need be said.

When all of a sudden

From out of the still night

There came such a ruckus

It gave such a fright.

As we glanced out the window

Like a shot from a gun

Several of us saw a wagon

Bouncing around while on the run.

The driver was whistling and singing with a will

The zebras (not reindeer)

He drove with such skill;

"Come all of you, black and white stripes!

Please, go far more to the right,

As there will be plenty of traveling

For you all tonight!"

The driver with a robe and a shirt that was red,

Also wore a red turban on top of his head.

As he stepped from his wagon

He really was a sight

With his head and mustache so curly and white.

As he burst into St. Julian's

Everyone awoke!

And all so astonished that none of the team spoke.

Then he filled up our footwear

With a present or two

That none of us could think what we should then do

When the mission team recovered the use of their jaws

Someone asked in a whisper,

"Are you Santa Claus?

"Am I the real Santa?

Well what do you think?

And he smiled as he gave

Us all a mysterious wink.

Then he leapt back on his wagon,

And he called back in his drawl,

"To all the people of Kenya,

Merry Christmas you all!"

*****

THE CLIMB BEGINS

Tuesday, Dec. 27th, 2005
Ascent, Mt. Kilimanjaro, Tanzania, Africa

Yesterday we left St. Julian's Centre and arrived in Arusha around 2:00 p.m., staying at Impala Hotel. What a hoot! Bob and Cheryl Combest-Friedman's room has a round bed!

On the beginning of the journey today, we came across a Coca-Cola truck with an advertisement on the back, "Follow me, and you will find refreshment." Immediately I thought of our Lord - reminded that I am a guest on this journey – a guest on the mountain!

Right now it's a bit too cloudy to see the mountain – at least that's what the driver says. To be honest, I am glad. I don't know if anyone else has butterflies in their stomach besides me. Butterflies! Perhaps that's not too bad because butterflies are the sign of new life! While I ponder my anxieties of the climb, Todd is talking to the driver about polygamy and why people in the western world only have one wife.

*****

THE FINAL ASCENT

Many school essays and college applications included the Kilimanjaro climb. Laina Combest-Friedman, the youngest member of the team, climbing at the age of twelve, wrote THE FINAL ASCENT for her 9th Grade English Class.

"We are suddenly awakened in our tents to begin the final ascent up Mt. Kilimanjaro. I look outside into the dark and see the glow of many small headlamps. A glance at my watch tells me that it is ten thirty – yes, ten thirty p.m. The strong wind blowing through our tent gives me the chills. After hours of walking earlier and only a few precious hours of sleep, I am not prepared to walk another 10 hours. It is below freezing, and I just want to go back to bed in my warm sleeping bag. Rubbing my eyes to keep awake, I gather my warm clothes to dress.

The guides tell us to wear all of our socks and as much as we can to keep warm. I pull on my long underwear, walking pants, and snow pants. I throw on my Under Armor®, fleece jacket, rain jacket and down coat. I put on 3 pairs of wool socks but have to take one pair off because my feet will not fit into my boots. Since it is pitch black, everyone must wear a headlamp. I grab my facemask and prepare myself to step outside into the cold.

Everyone is gathered around listening intently to the guides speak about tonight's climb. They say to try and drink as little water as possible and go "pole, pole", which means slowly in Swahili. I guess that there is some concern that the water might freeze in our stomachs, or if too much is consumed, cause us to be sick. Porters hand out some snacks for the climb. After some delicious cookies and tea, I grab my daypack and I am ready to leave.

The altitude is around 16,000 as we begin to climb, and I feel sick to my stomach already. I keep wondering how I am going to do this. Will I make it to the summit or at least to the top? I am trying to keep positive thoughts. I tell myself that I am going to make it to the summit and that this climb will not be very hard. I decide that I will just keep moving at a slow pace. I begin walking in one of the last groups to start the ascent with my sister, two other girls, and one of the lead guides named Stanley. I feel like I am going to throw up, but I am determined to keep going. I did not come this far to give up now! Dropping to my knees for a rest, I get sick. Stanley rushed to my side to comfort me. "Are you okay?" he asks. I tell him that I feel much better. Now that I feel somewhat recovered, I can walk faster. Stanley assigns one of the porters to take me ahead.

Many challenges lie ahead as we slowly ascend. Walking on this steep slope of shale is difficult and my porter is no help. My feet slip slightly on the shale with each step I take. The porter is walking too fast for me to keep up. I feel sick again, and I am extremely tired. The porter doesn't speak English and it is very frustrating for me that he keeps walking and does not look back to check on me. I could be halfway down the mountain and he would not have a clue. I drop to my knees to see if he even notices. The porter keeps walking for a while and finally sees that I am not behind him. He stops until I get up. As soon as I get up, he walks ahead of me. I drop to my knees often to rest, and, at this point, I urgently need a big rock to shield me for a bathroom break. Fortunately, my porter stops to talk with a guide.

I slowly walk up to the two men and ask, *"Is there a place where I can go to the bathroom?"*

The guide replies, *"bafroom? You want bafroom?"* As he sweeps his hand across the landscape, he says, *"You got annnnnywhere you want."*

I could see with the small glow of my headlamp a few gravel-size rocks to the side of the trail. I can hear people coming behind me. I am too worn out and tired to care. I just hope that they don't shine their light towards me! As I walked back to the guide and the porter, the guide takes me ahead. After a few minutes of walking, we catch up to the large group in the front. I can hear my oldest sister and her friend talking above me. I can see my dad, my brother and his friend. There are many other people making the climb as well. The next thing I remember is falling again to my knees and getting sick.

Guides rush over to comfort me. I could hear my sister in the background asking "Is that Laina?" The guides tell me that I should turn around and go back down to camp. In my mind, I am saying there is no way that I am turning back! My dad and brother come down to join me. The guide tells my dad that I should probably return as this is the second time that I have been sick. They are worried that if I climb further I might suffer from severe altitude sickness. After talking to my dad, the guide decides to let me continue with the knowledge that if I get sick again, I will have to return to camp. I am upset since I have come so far and certainly do not want to turn around.

After getting through these few hurdles, I am more determined than ever to make it to the top of this mountain. My dad, brother, and I stay together. We are given a new guide to take us to the top. My feet are frozen and I can barely feel my toes. I still drop to rest every few minutes. Each time, I push myself another minute before I fall to the ground for another rest. Why am I doing this to myself? Why am I torturing my body? I could be at home sitting by a warm fire sleeping. Being back in the tent sleeping even sounds like heaven now. I don't know why but I do know that I will do anything to get to the top of this mountain.

My guide doesn't like me resting so often, and I am starting to feel badly for my dad, brother and the guide. I cause them to stop every few minutes to wait for me. My guide is worried that if I rest for too long, I will freeze, and won't be able to go on. I repeatedly tell him that I am not going to freeze, and I beg for one more minute of rest. Since I am incredibly tired and sick, my guide has taken my daypack and poles. He stands in front of me and takes my hands. He puts my hands in his coat pockets to keep them warm. As we walk, he pulls me behind him. I am practically sleeping while being dragged up this mountain. I rest my head on his back and slowly drag one foot in front of the other.

To save energy for walking, the guides don't want us to talk. Melodious sounds drift across the wide expanse of the mountain as the guides sing in Swahili to entertain us while walking. I see a big shiny light that doesn't look that far away. We must be close to the top! As I continually drop to rest, I get sick again. I ask my guide and my dad if I may continue. I promised that if I threw up one more time, I would go back down. I am not religious and I don't pray; but I am now praying to God countless times. Suddenly we stop. I collapse on the ground, excited that I have reached the top! I go to my brother, and he tells me that this is just a ten-minute break and that we still have a few more hours ahead of us. I am so disappointed! How am I going to make it? I find a rock to rest on.

I am abruptly wakened. *"Laina, get up!"* *"We need to keep moving."* I take a few minutes to get up, and then head off. I feel tremendously weak. I stop to have a tiny sip of water.

"I can't feel my toes," I exclaim to my guide.

He unties my boots, and rubs my feet until they feel a little warmer. I keep seeing this big light, but we have walked for hours and still have not reached it yet. Since I am so weak, my guide literally picks me up, and places me on the rocks we are climbing. My guide keeps saying, *"You are almost there, don't give up."* After a couple hours of climbing rocks, we come to a stop.

My brother is enormously enthusiastic. *"Laina, we made it, I am so proud of you."* I cannot believe what I am hearing! I am so excited that the first thing I do is find a place to sit and collapse. I am freezing, full of frost, and it is snowing. After about five minutes of sleep, my guide wakes me up and says, *"Are you ready to go to the summit?"*

I was blown away! Here I thought I had made it to the summit. He says that they consider Gilman's Point the top. We are at Gilman's Point, but the summit is about another two hours away. I can see the glaciers from where I am standing. There really is nothing else. My dad tells the guide that the top is fine for us; we will head back down.

The ascent up Mount Kilimanjaro, the highest mountain on the continent of Africa, is over! I have made it to the top just as the sun begins to rise. The only thing left now is the descent and the memories that will stay with me for a lifetime. As we head down the mountain, I am feeling a little better. I am so proud of myself for making it to the top after all I have been through.

Heading down the mountain is a heck of a lot easier than walking up in this shale. The sun is coming out, and it is getting hot. I start to peel off layer after layer of my clothing. Now that I can see what I climbed, I wonder how many people would attempt to climb something so steep. As we quickly descend, my dad, brother, and I frequently turn to look up at the mountain, so proud of what we have accomplished.

It has taken a great deal of determination, something I didn't know I possessed until now. I believe now I can accomplish anything if I put my mind to it. Back at camp, I collapse onto a rock and lay my head on my lap falling into a deep sleep with the sun beating down on one side of my face. I will wake up tomorrow ready to walk another twelve miles to the end. I know these twelve miles will be nothing, as I can accomplish anything!"

*****

LESSONS LEARNED ALONG THE WAY
By Charese McGregor, age 15

"It was 4:17 a.m. Although covered by a ski mask in the charcoal darkness, my disappointment was still quite visible. My blood-shot eyes looked back to the mountain I had attempted to conquer.

The porter suggested to my parents and sister that I not continue my assent, otherwise there may be serious health

issues and possibly death. Slowly I descended, trying to with-
hold the salt water from rushing down my cheeks. But one tear
escaped, and then another, and soon I could feel the onset of
a migraine. Extreme altitude and lack of oxygen at 19,000 feet
had turned a common cold into a very dangerous situation.
Nothing was going the way I had planned.

Arriving back at the morning's base camp, I walked into
the tent that had become so familiar to me the past five days.
Protected from extreme elements of wind and cold, I picked
up a pen and tried to write, but my fingers were as frozen as the
glacier above. Writing my experience of climbing the mountain
would not take place at that moment. The pen fell from my
hand and within moments I fell into a deep sleep.

When I awoke, pure reality hit me. I had just climbed Mt.
Kilimanjaro, the highest freestanding mountain in the world.
Through my Kilimanjaro adventure in Tanzania, Africa, I realized that even though I only needed a few hundred more feet
to make it to the top, I *had* persevered until the end. With every
bit of energy I put into that night, I realized the true meaning
of perseverance. I am assured that when I face another great
challenge in life, I will remember to give every effort I have.
The final destination is not always the most important part of
our journey, but the lessons we learn along the way."

*****

HAPPY NEW YEAR!

New Years Day – 2006 –
Descent, Mt. Kilimanjaro, Tanzania, Africa

Climbing Kili was the most challenging physical feat I have ever accomplished or attempted. All 24 people in our group would agree – it took each one of us every ounce of determination, perseverance, and energy we could grasp from inside out. We walked 36 miles in 6 days, 40 hours of walking in 140 hours. We could have never done it without each other and the porters and guides.

In preparation for climbing Mt. Kilimanjaro, I had dreamed of how I would reach the top and bask in the joy of being on top of Africa's highest mountain. But after an arduous journey, working my weary bones to make it to the rim of the crater at over 19,000 feet high, I crawled on all fours to the plaque that read "Gillman's Point", gave it a brief glance and anticipated my journey down. Drinking tea from a tin cup the guides had carried up the mountain, I sat on top of Africa and stared absently at the vastness around. Numb from hard work, cold and emotion, I was blank. The detour had brought me to an altitude of almost 20,000 feet, and all I wanted to do was go back to camp.

*****

WE CLIMBED UP MT. KILI

On the bus, after the climb, we wrote the following song to the tune of "On top of Old Smoky."

WE CLIMBED UP MT. KILI

We climbed up Mt. Kili
24 people in a row
They said 'pole-pole'
You must go very slow

    After Christmas in Kenya
    We arrived at Rongai
    They're waiting to greet us
    57 cooks, porters and guides

Day one: We saw rainforest monkeys
And put gaiters on
Though hot, dirty and dusty
Our team began to bond.

    Day two: Was not easy
    As we began to climb
    Diamox affecting our bladder
    And the altitude, our mind.

Day Three: Just to acclimatize
We thought we'd relax
But after a "short walk"
We hit our tents and collapsed

Day four: Came the real ascent

Alpine desert and Kibo Huts

With the mountain looming in front of us

We began to go nuts.

This was the longest day

We we'll have more than one verse

To tell all our stories

Leaving deo and purse.

Beginning before midnight

With cookies and tea

Our guides told us not to drink

It was too cold to go pee

How will we make it?

One step at a time

Hakuna Matata

It begins in the mind

The moments were grueling

Our steps were so slow

Through shale and steep incline

Our feet would not go.

Some got to the summit

And others to the top

But even those who attempted

Give up, they did not.

Some ran down the mountain

Others sat down to rest

But all of our team members

Gave it their best.

Day 5: But arriving at Kibo

We could not rest

Push on to the next camp

Just more of the test

    New Years Eve is upon us

    And what did we do?

    15 youth – did they party?

    No. Barely took off their shoes (boots!)

Day 6: Sleep in the next morning?

It's now New Years day!

Ha, Ha, that is funny

Twenty km and sunrays

    Knees wobbling and blisters

    Finally back at the gate

    What gave strength to finish?

    It must have been fate.

A short celebration

Team pictures to boot

People selling t-shirts

And much other loot.

    After our tradition of high 5's

    We ended in prayer

    For this was the reason

    To show that we care.

We're People Reaching People

And want others to know

Sharing love, hope and unity

We'll watch our faith grow.

*****

FAMILY REUNION

When we were back to our hotel rooms, showered and had a drink and hot meal, we shared Christ-like Moments. It was clear that building community and interdependence was a common theme. Throughout the walk, we all continued in fellowship encouraging each other to continue one step at a time. However, some of us didn't talk as much as anticipated. It depleted too much oxygen!

Our group was impressed in the teamwork between the porters and guides. They were a great group of people and it was clear that for many, it was not just a job, but a passion to lead others up the highest mountain in Africa. Team members that did not know one another previous to the Kilimanjaro climb were impressed by the fact that people can come into your life for just six days and get to know one another because they were pushing (and pulling!) others up the mountain. A team member commented, *"One person influenced me more in a few days than some others I've known for a lifetime!"*

Once back in bus, it was like a family reunion. Celebration drinks, high-fives and songs of merriment. We will never be the same. Deeper in relationships we laid aside "personal boundaries" and found the core of our teammates through helping one another through trying circumstances. Certainly, these were precious moments. As one climber states, *"There were no arguments in group. I was definitely very irritated climbing the mountain, but everybody got along!"*

*****

NOT SOMETHING YOU WANT TO DO TWICE

January 2nd, 2006
Impala Hotel, Tanzania

Life has a much different viewpoint depending on the circumstances around us. Now that we have arrived back at the hotel, guzzled a cold drink, relished a swim in the pool, appreciated a hot shower, and consumed a hot meal my mind plays tricks on me. As I lay my head on the feather pillow, I ponder and ask myself, "Why didn't you push yourself just a little harder to go from the top to the summit?" Honestly, physically, I didn't have it in me. Another three hours to the summit could have put me over the edge. Would it have been worth it?

Our mind does this to us, doesn't it? When we have accomplished such a great feat, we still have gluttony for more instead of being satisfied with what we accomplished. On the treadmill of success, we always want more.

It was just one week ago today when we arrived at this hotel. Before the climb, we had such high expectations. Even though the hill outside our bedroom window looked a challenge to climb, we were all going to make it to the top. We anticipated twenty-four people at the summit for a picture on UHURU Peak. Piers brought a golf club with 5 balls to hit into the crater, which he did with Julian and Brian. All our gear was strategically packed; thirty-five pounds for the porter to carry and daypacks we carried ourselves. We were ready to conquer the mountain.

As Todd said, the climb gives us a new respect for nature. At 19,340 feet, life has a different perspective. Not only can clouds roll in quickly, but so can acute mountain sickness, cerebral edema. Vomiting and diarrhea can consume a person's mind and body and make it impossible to reach the top. During our descent from Kibo hut to Mandara, a porter was medically evacuated for acute mountain sickness. One large bicycle wheel and a few planks of wood held a man's life. Strapped in a sleeping bag, five fellow porters sprinted their teammate down the mountain to descend as quickly as possible. Timing was imperative. Every minute mattered. He wasn't a novice. The porter had been up the mountain several times before. "It can happen to any of us, at any time," Stanley, our guide stated. "One never knows what will happen on the mountain."

Human beings try to conquer nature. We try to overcome the natural forces of gravity and altitude and go thousands of feet above and below sea level. And for what is our purpose? This is the answer for which I am still searching. Perhaps it is the quest for life. But as an RVA student explained of her climb of Mt. Kili *"It is not something you want to do twice!"*

*****

THE QUEST

At first I, Patsy, would describe our Kili mission as an "adventure." But author Kevin Ford describes the difference between adventure and quest. "The majority recommends we stay with the status quo, the safe and easy paths of adventure, and ignore the dangerous roads of quest. Quest changes a person. They are the things that make a person great. It is, in fact, the experience of failure and the crucible of adversity that shape us."[ii] Quest is a step further than adventure – it is being transformed.

Truly, our team members were on a quest. "Anticipate that pain will come prior to the reward. Of course, this is how life works: childbirth before we can hold the newborn; darkness before dawn; discipline before high grades; and the Cross before the Resurrection."[iii] And may I add, the ardent climb before reaching the top.

*****

BRAVO – TO ALL OF US!

On the car ride back, we couldn't take our eyes off the mountain and what we had climbed! Bravo – to all of us!"

LESSONS LEARNED ALONG THE DETOUR:

If I had never gone on my off-road safari to work in Kenya, I would never have accomplished the great feat of climbing Mt. Kilimanjaro. Some off-road experiences we may not want to do twice, but certainly we may have been challenged by the quest! At 19,340 feet, life has a different perspective. Is there a feat you have accomplished that now gives you a sense of great purpose? How are you learning that, with God's help, you can do all things through Christ who strengthens you?

DETOUR PRAYER:

Lord, help us to consider it pure joy whenever we face trials because we know that the testing of our faith develops perseverance and perseverance must finish its work so that we may be mature and complete, not lacking anything. (James 1:2-4) Give us assurance and knowledge that suffering does produce perseverance, perseverance character; and character, hope. And hope does not disappoint us because God has poured out His love into our hearts by the Holy Spirit, whom he has given us. Therefore, we rejoice in the hope of the glory of God. (Rom 5:2-5)

CHAPTER FIVE

MARS....A....BIT

"The desert tribes will bow before him
and his enemies will lick the dust." Ps. 72:9

CONSIDER THE COST

St. Patrick's Day, Friday, March 17th, 2006.
Nairobi, Kenya

Today I fly to Marsabit. Todd is already there and from
Marsabit we will drive eight hours to the Ethiopian border, to
Moyale. Sunday we will go to church and then we will drive
back.

To say the least, I am not looking forward to it. Why am
I doing it? To be a support to my husband. But can the Lord
change this stubborn heart? Can He cause me to have a more
willing spirit? Can He mold me more into the image of Christ?
I know He can, and therefore, I surrender.

E. Stanley Jones describes the activity of God and the response of His children in the establishment and cultivation of conversion as a "delicate balance." Conversion is "a gift and an achievement, the act of a moment and the work of a lifetime...constantly enlarge the area of your conversion. Make your conversion take in more and more of your life."[iv]

Some of our conversions are "Conversions Limited," and some are "Conversions, Unlimited." Is this the same with missionaries and missionary service? "Missionaries Limited and "Missionaries Unlimited." It is a thought-provoking evaluation.

It is up in the airplane that I feel most alone. This six-seater prop engine does not allow for chatter. For two hours I have only my own contemplations. No cell phones or computers. My mind goes in a billion different directions. Where is my focus?

I realize that I must give up the habits that cannot be Christianized. I know I slow down my Christian progress just by a few habits that are not "so bad" but neither "so good." Is my lack of excitement in going to Northern Kenya one of these bad habits? 2 Peter 1:5-7 states, "For this very reason, make every effort to add to your faith goodness; and to goodness, knowledge; and to knowledge, self-control; and to self-control, perseverance; and to perseverance, godliness; and to godliness, brotherly kindness; and to brotherly kindness, love." Supplement means add to something to the faith that is already there. Lord, increase my faith.

Paul reminds us in Philippians 2:12, to "continue to work out your salvation with fear and trembling," I think I have some work to do.

*****

ARE YOU WILLING?

Saturday, March 18th, 2006
Marsabit, Northern Kenya

Heavy sigh. This is not an easy life up here. No water. Bucket baths – with one cup cold water and one cup hot water. Considering what they (Todd, actually) had to do to bring me that one cup was quite a task! For $200.00 USD they trucked in a heavy tanker of water! Then they put it in the big tank, heated it up with firewood and a half hour later – hot water! Lord, grace me with the gift of gratitude.

Things are progressing slowly here in the north. At least for the meantime, Todd feels led to come up here. The Archbishop has spoken several times of consecrating Todd as Assistant Missionary Bishop. This is an exciting opportunity for him. Then why do I sit on this bed crying?

I remember how hard our years were in Madagascar. Yes, ten best years of our lives, but a challenging ten nevertheless with many ups and downs. God wants us to be at the place where we can say 'Yes' to whatever he wants to bring us. Why am I so hesitant to come here? Why is my response back to the Lord a prolonged 'yyyyeeeeeeessssss'?

I guess I am considering the cost. It wasn't easy for me to even get up and go to the restroom this morning! With my strained knee, it is difficult to squat. Try that sometime – using a pit latrine standing up! And then there is that smell!

Secondly, there are no other ex-pats living here permanently. Yesterday I saw a few UN and EU people who are up here because of drought and famine. There was also a group from Texas working with Food for the Hungry - but a common friend with whom to chat and have a cup of coffee? I would have to rely on my husband and long distance phone calls back to Nairobi.

Consider the cost. Are you willing?

In my quest to "succeed" and "better my life" it seems a dichotomy to "take up His cross" and follow Him to the desert regions of the North.

Yesterday, on the six-seater Cessna, I vomited just getting here. We thank God for the clouds that might bring rain, but that then brings air currents….

Today in our eight hour, hot dusty drive to the Ethiopian border we are to take an armed guard. There has been a fair amount of cattle rustling going on lately and the gun might prevent bandits.

Consider the cost. Are you willing?

In my vision, I want to help bring people to the place of willingness. I believe God is calling us to host short-term mission groups and give them the opportunity to hand over their lives to the Lord in service to Him. But in order to lead others, I have to be willing to go there myself.

Consider the cost. Are you willing?

Over the past year, I have wanted to begin my second book. Ever since I stepped foot onto the grounds at St. Julian's Centre, I wanted to entitle it "At Home in Africa." Now, after knowing the possibility of moving to Marsabit, I am not so sure. Will this ever become home?

E. Stanley Jones encourages us to "constantly enlarge the area of your conversion." Richard Foster challenges us: "Make your conversion take in more and more areas of your life."[v] How can I do this today? Tomorrow? In the days to come?

*****

A ROADSIDE RECESS

Same day: 12:45 p.m.
Turbi, Northern Kenya

We have stopped for a bite to eat in Turbi, a village on the route to Ethiopia, on the side of a hill. Todd has mentioned that there are several less villagers due to the massacre last year when more than 100 people were killed, including 28 children at the local school. The Borana came over from Ethiopia and partook in their own ethnic cleansing against the Gabbra – many of them women and children.

They have just delivered my pilau and goat meat. In a timely manner the wind blew my journal to another page – which in bold letters was written – "TASTE AND SEE THAT THE LORD IS GOOD."

This pilau is a bit different than I expected. Hmm, oh well, the coke is cold. I gave it up for Lent – but not today. On the sign of the tin shack shop is a hand painted sign with a *Coke* bottle and advertisement stating "This is the bounty of the Lord." I figure today is a day of celebration that I am even here. Today, I will forgo my Lenten discipline and celebrate my willingness to follow the Lord to the uttermost parts of the earth.

Another reason there are fewer people is because of less traffic. That sounds funny here in the middle of the desert, but this is the only road Cape Town to Cairo. People, truckers mainly, no longer come this way. If they want to go to the Ethiopian border or Moyale, where we are headed today, they drive several miles out of the way - to Wajir and Garrisa, not through this town, Turbi, because of the bandits. I am glad we have an armed guard. We decided to come this way because we wanted to stop at a few villages "on the way" – which are actually more out of the way than on the way to Ethiopia. Uran and Sololo will be two of our stops.

On the way to Turbi, we stopped in Bubisa and distributed food transported last night by a truck from Marsabit - 25 large jugs of oil, 140 bags of maize and 60 sacks of beans. Each woman representing her family received seven cups of maize and three of beans. St. Julian's Centre donated KSH 25,000/- (approximately $350) toward the project and friends from the UK have the other donations. I distributed the food hand in hand with Bishop Waqo.

*****

SHIFTAS

Same day, 3:45 p.m.
Sololo, Northern Kenya

Now we are in a Borana village just on the boarder of Ethiopia. The first words from the villagers described a recent (yesterday's) attack of the Gabbra just a few kilometers away. No one was killed or hurt, but several animals stolen.

Carcasses dot the road everywhere. One can actually smell the stench of death. But thank God for the rain they have had – the first in three years for some – and we have seen the hand of the government getting involved…drilling four boreholes and more police blockages to keep the *shiftas* (bandits) away.

I think the challenge for me as an individual is how to be equally content in both environments. Can I be equally comfortable and content sitting in this half-built church on a hard bench with women in headscarves saying "Ngeni badada"(their traditional greeting) than sitting poolside in a comfortable lounge chair with tea brought to my side?

Consider the cost.

Someone walks toward me with an empty pail and a cup of water so that I can wash my hands before eating the ugali (dried corn meal somewhat like unseasoned grits!), gizzards and liver they have so graciously prepared for us. How long did they have to walk to get the water they so elaborately poured over my hands? I would rather eat the bag of peanuts I stashed in my purse just in case we got stranded roadside. Would I offend them by leaving the liver and gizzards (which are a delicacy) on the plate and put out my bag of peanuts? I decided not to take a chance and saved the peanuts for later.

It's interesting to notice that three local villagers around this table are wearing People Reaching People shirts. Sometimes during a hard day it's nice to remember that by the grace of God, we are making a difference. The eldest Christian in the village, Paul Guyo, is here. He was abandoned by his parents, and denied inheritance. Naiomi, Bishop Waqo's wife, wrote about him in her Master's thesis. The story displays the clash between the culture and the gospel.

*****

SCHOOL DEBATES

Same day, 5:10 p.m.

We continue to meet with people and have now stopped at a secondary school in Uran. I wander around the village while Todd and Bishop Waqo discuss church issues with local congregants. I decide to talk to the teachers and begin conversation.

What do people study at your school?

They lead me over to a torn piece of paper glued to a wooden plank that served as a wall. Listed are some of the subjects the 12 year-old students debate at the school in Uran every Wednesday afternoon. I copied them in my journal.

1. To educate a girl is better than to educate a boy.
2. Female genital mutilation should be encouraged (Health is better than wealth).
3. Drug Abuse – taking alcohol should be legalized.
4. Environment – cutting down trees for timber should be allowed.
5. HIV/AIDS – The HIV/AIDS patient should be isolated.
6. Gender – a girl is equivalent to a boy.
7. Poverty – relief supply should be discouraged.
8. Illiteracy – illiterate is better than literacy.

9. Sexuality – should abortion be legalized?
10. Morality – sex before marriage.
11. Relationship – a neighbor is better than family.
12. Life – living in outskirts is better than living in town.
13. Modern technology – is it helpful?

The current class is smart. 80.65% passed the KCPE performance exams (equivalent to passing into the next grade) and were awarded a goat by Bishop Waqo. There was one girl in the final class of 22 boys. As the students get older, the numbers of girls in the class decrease. Out of 495 students, 299 are boys and 196 are girls with only nine teachers. The problem is that when the girl becomes an adolescent and breaks blood, she no longer comes to school when she has her period. Thus, one week out of every month, since they cannot afford methods of sanitary hygiene, the girl is not able to study in class and misses out on a great deal of learning.

After talking to the teachers, I tried conversing with some Level 8 boys studying English.

Do you like your school? Yes

Do you like to study? Yes

Do you like your teacher? Yes

Do you always answer yes? Yes (with great big smiles)

*****

ETHIOPIAN BORDER

Sunday, March 19th, 2006

Moyale, Kenya, bordering Southern Ethiopian

Thoughts of a deacon (me!) during what turned out to be a 5 ½ hour service, in two foreign languages: Bishop Waqo spoke in Kiswahili and another priest translated into Borana. In that one service, there were:

- confirmation of 4 candidates
- opening of a nursery school
- commissioning of six evangelists
- Holy Communion for 500 people
- Blessing of six couples' marriages

Back to yesterday's thoughts of being comfortable in both environments; lying poolside with tea served to my side or sitting on a cracked cement block underneath an acacia tree in the middle of the Chelbi desert.

Are we called to comfort? Are we called to focus on our own needs or the needs of others? Are we called to "fit" in? Peter calls God's elect "strangers in the world" who were "chosen according to the foreknowledge of God." (1 Peter 1:1-2) If I am truly convinced that prayer changes things, if I truly believe that I can make a difference in the world just by intercession, then it would not matter where I pray – by the pool, in the lovely garden at St. Julian's Centre or in the middle of the Northern Kenya desert!

Paul writes that he "was called to be an apostle and set apart for the gospel of God". (Romans 1:1) John says he was "sent from God as a witness to testify concerning that light so that through him all men might believe." (John 1:6-8)

Are we confident enough to fulfill our calling?

Obadiah wrote his vision
Jonah proclaimed to the people of Nineveh
Habakkuk received an oracle
Zephaniah heard the word of the Lord
Mary responded to the angel
Esther obeyed with boldness

Would I be confident in my own calling to proclaim:

The Word of the Lord to the Anglican Church of Kenya (ACK)?

The Word of the Lord to Todd concerning Northern Kenya?

How confident is my walk with the Lord?

What about Todd and thoughts of him becoming a Missionary Bishop in Northern Kenya? Can we be assured that he is "sent not from men nor by man, but by Jesus Christ and

God the Father?" Can we be assured that it is not just the ACK who is zealous for development within their own institution?

If so, what are they expecting out of a Bishop's wife? Someone who sits at the cathedral, doing crochet with the Mothers Union? That's fine if that is the call of God upon the wife. But I see my role as different – more as an ambassador between the rich and the poor – the "reached" and the "unreached." I see myself as a bridge between "overdeveloped" and "developing" countries…those who live in million-dollar homes on the ocean and those who live in closet-sized huts made out of cattle dung and sticks.

There has been so much talk of Todd becoming Bishop. It's played our minds like a yo-yo. The church must first decide – "who is your man?" 1 Cor. 1:18-31. ACK: "Who is your man to become Bishop"?

If you recognize his gifts and desire him to serve you as a Missionary Bishop, do you also recognize my gifts and talents as being an ambassador of the Lord? What do we do with St. Julian's and the fellowship of believers meeting there on Sunday?

If we do decide to serve the Lord in Northern Kenya, it is of course inevitable that some people will just not understand. They will think we are foolish. "For the message of the cross is foolishness to those who are perishing, but to us who are being saved it is the power of God." (1 Cor. 1:18, 22) "Jews demand miraculous signs and Greeks look for wisdom (and Americans search for wealth and success) but we preach Christ crucified.

But we stand strong on 1 Cor. 1:25 "For the foolishness of God is wiser than man's wisdom and the weakness of God is stronger than man's strength."

My thoughts continue during this somewhat long church service. Dotted by humor that Todd's chair broke when he sat on it! Bishop Waqo's sermon began at 1:35 p.m. – four hours after the service began! Remember the peanuts stashed away in my purse? I thanked God for them and slipped out for a small snack and to rid myself of the tea I had that morning.

But it is a powerful sermon. He says "the role of the church is to not speak here at the pulpit but to transform society in every realm – we are ambassadors of Christ in all aspects of life. Initiate peace and reconciliation especially here in Northern Kenya."

The word of the Bishop is to 'encourage people not to be complacent but to move!'

Where is God moving us?

*****

ON THE ROAD AGAIN

Monday, March 20th, 2006
In the truck, driving with an armed guard from Moyale to Marsabit.

So what is God saying to us about Northern Kenya?

Go…strategically?

Go…creatively?

Go…realistically?

Is Mars…a…bit another off-road safari? When will I just get to recline in my limousine and enjoy the easy road of life?

*****

UNEVENTFUL ROAD TRIP

Tuesday, March 21, 2006, Marsabit

Our 12-hour drive yesterday was relatively "uneventful" – Praise be to God. We stopped in Walda to talk to the people who moved from Turbi because of the raid where over 100 people – many women and children— were massacred. They were on the outskirts of the town. It was our desire to talk to the chief and praise be to God, both the chief and the District Officer were there! God is good!

When talking with them they did confirm that three people were killed on Friday in another village not too far away – another cattle raid. It is really unsettling to the people up here and more Kenyan police have been stationed here. Soldiers carrying machine guns escort almost every car. One woman, working with UK Tear Fund, is carrying TWO security guards with her!

Today I am flying back to Nairobi – Todd is staying on for three more days and fixing up the house that we will be living in when we come here (with or without the purple shirt.) I have a St. Julian's Staff retreat and as a group, we drive to Nakuru.

My mind continues the battle and the challenge remains. How do I become content in both environments? Leading a "nomadic" life style, traveling back and forth every few weeks to Marsabit, could be extremely draining! Why would anyone in their right minds move to rural Marsabit? Imagine if I were house hunting in the States. Not only would I look at the house itself, but also the road (which of course, would be paved), the accessibility to shops, school, church and driving distance to various convenience spots. Actually, much of what we would look for would be convenience.

On the contrary here! What does it take to live in Marsabit?

A flight (not a road) to get here

A free-for-all dumping area just outside the compound

A market – with blaring amplifier – on the other side of our fence

A small house with a porch view looking onto a latrine

All of which are out of my control!

I must remember that even though I can't choose what is outside the house – or my environment – I can choose what I put inside my house.

It reminds me perhaps of a woman born with a birth defect – even perhaps to her face. That person has no control over how she was born – with or without defect, but she has a daily choice on how to live and what to put inside her heart. Will she live with resentment or bitterness? Will she be burdened with resentment every time she looks in the mirror? Or will she thank God for the privilege to be alive and then choose her thoughts wisely?

Wise living with a grateful heart is my choice today. I will choose to live a life that matters.

*****

I have a stash of inspirational poems that I have picked up along the way. I don't know anything about this author, and his circumstances but his poem reminds us that living a life that matters doesn't happen by accident. It's not a matter of circumstances, but of choice.

WHAT WILL IT MATTER?
By Michael Josephson

Ready or not, some day it will all come to an end.
There will be no more sunrises, no minutes, hours or days.

All the things you collected, whether treasured or forgotten,

will pass to someone else.

Your wealth, fame and temporal power will

shrivel to irrelevance.

It will not matter what you owned or what you were owed.

Your grudges, resentments, frustrations and jealousies will

finally disappear.

So too, your hopes, ambitions, plans and

to-do lists will expire.

The wins and losses that once seemed so important

will fade away.

It won't matter where you come from or what side of the

tracks you lived on at the end

It won't matter whether you were beautiful or brilliant.

Even your gender and skin color will be irrelevant.

So what WILL matter? How will the value of your

days be measured?

What will matter is not what you bought but what you built,

not what you got but what you gave.

What will matter is not your success but your significance.

What will matter is not what you learned but what you taught.

What will matter is every act of integrity, compassion,

courage or sacrifice that enriched, empowered or encouraged

others to emulate your example.

What will matter is not your competence but your character.
What will matter is not how many people you knew, but how
many will feel a lasting loss when you're gone.
What will matter is not YOUR memories but the memories
of those who loved you.
What will matter is how long you will be remembered, but
whom and for what.

Living a life what matters doesn't happen by accident.
It's not a matter of circumstance but of choice.
Choose to live a life that matters.

*****

THINKING FOR A CHANGE

"Conscious repentance leads to unconscious holiness."
Oswald Chambers

Now that I accept the idea that we might be called to live in
Northern Kenya (at least part of the time), how do I choose to
live my life in order to embrace the call God has placed upon
me through Christ Jesus? In order to live up to the calling I
have received – as Paul writes in Eph. 4:1, I need to come up
with a strategic plan on how to think.

In the most current book I am reading, *Thinking for a Change*,
John Maxwell encourages us to think differently. "Is my desire

for success and to improve my life strong enough to prompt me to change my thinking?"[vi] Now that I examine my own thinking, I see that my idea of success and improvement has – if even so subtly – been based on "western thinking."

- a lovely home
- good car
- nice neighborhood
- fine schools
- money for the future
- money for today

But here I am living life so differently...called to live apart from the ways of the world and to take up my cross and follow him. Why do we always think of the cross as difficult? Do we only think of the suffering and crucifixion or about the celebration and resurrection afterwards?

"If you want to <u>live</u> on a new level, you need to <u>think</u> on a new level."[vii] In the past, I have based so much of my thinking on the physical. Physical environment, physical food, physical home, physical office, physical appearance...

But now I realize that in order to <u>thrive</u> I need to think differently.

Maxwell questions his readers,

"Do you want to succeed where you have failed before? Do you want to go to a level you never dreamed possible? Do you want to become the person you always hoped you could be? If you do, don't start by trying to change your actions, start by changing your mind."[viii]

Is my desire for success (happiness on the mission field) and to improve my life strong enough to prompt me to change my thinking?

These past two years at St. Julian's have been good years, full of growth in so many ways: Growth in managerial skills, self-confidence, staff relationships, problem solving, and leadership skills including staff devotions and worship. Praise God for all of these areas of growth! My spiritual life has developed. I see areas in which I have been strengthened and areas which I would like to develop.

For example, I have been strengthened by leading staff devotions several times a week. The ACK (Anglican Church of Kenya) has prepared me to lead a church body and I have gained skills needed for ordination. I have enjoyed leading worship and have become stronger and confident with my voice. Personally, I have developed as an individual, gaining independence, not over-dependence on Todd. I seek wisdom and have become more confident and vision-minded. I focus less on myself and give more time to intercessory prayer.

However, with my new roles and responsibility, I have found that I don't write in my journal nearly as often and

secondly, I am more irregular in personal quiet time and God
– it's based more on devotions for staff – not myself.

All in all, this is good and is part of my role and responsibility as leader of St. Julian's Centre. However, to allow staff
devotions to fulfill my own intimate relationship with Christ
can be spiritually dangerous. Therefore, I set the goal to be in
the Word more and keep a journal of my spiritual growth.

*****

THINKING DIFFERENTLY

When I have tried to improve my life in the past, I have
begun with my own performance (something I can control)
and then gone to behavior, attitude, expectations, belief and
finally, thinking. But now I have learned that I have gone about
all of this backwards! I now see that in order to get to the
next level (even in our missionary life) I must FIRST THINK
differently because:

Thinking determines beliefs
Beliefs determine expectations
Expectations determine attitude
Attitudes determine behavior
Behavior determines performance
Performance determines my life![ix]

All the while, we must remember our biggest purpose in life: "To love the Lord our God with all our heart, soul and mind and our neighbor as ourself." (Luke 10:27)

One thing I derive from our experience in Madagascar is reflection. If I were to do it again, what would I do differently? What would I change or improve? How do I need to think differently in order to improve the next situation? What did I like? What did I dislike? Maxwell encourages us to engage in reflective thinking to enhance our own thinking patterns.

Jules Henri Poincare says: "To doubt everything or to believe everything are two equally convenient solutions; both dispense with the necessity of reflection." Let me apply this to my own situation: "To doubt that I can go to Northern Kenya or to believe that I can go easily are two equally convenient solutions; both dispense with the necessity of reflection." In order to flourish on the mission field I need to reflectively think on the past and present in order to thrive in the future.

"By mentally visiting past situations you can think with greater understanding. Reflective thinking is like the crock-pot of the mind. It encourages your thoughts to simmer until they are done."[x]

*****

LIFE IS NOT A BEACH

Tuesday, April 4th, 2006

In the air, flying from Nairobi to Marsabit

Instead of going to the beach for the girls' spring vacation, like many missionaries in Nairobi, we're going to the desert – Marsabit! Life is a challenge. It is a challenge to be nomadic, transient, living in two places. We are setting up home in Marsabit, and it is difficult. I feel like I just got settled at St. Julian's Centre.

And then there is the journey to get here! We could not take off at 9:00 a.m. this morning due to fog so we are flying in the small plane instead. We had to re-arrange the luggage a few times. We brought 60 kg and were allowed 80 kg so we went off to the store and bought dishes – a 47-piece set! That came to 19.87 kg. I thought we were exact weight for the Cessna – but then they told me later to take 10 kg out…so I took off my jacket and substituted the dish rack and a few more things…having the attitude "Oh well, whatever…" then, when we changed planes again, I could wear my jacket again and could have taken the raisins and granola but I thought I couldn't so I LEFT THEM IN THE CAR! Ugh! Oh Well, whatever! I am here, in the air. It seems like I did this just yesterday. Actually, I did it last week.

All alone…far from home
    In the sky…way up high
Alone with my thoughts
    To ponder and think
And put paper together with ink

Take me away
    To another world
Freedom…take me out of the box
    And allow my thoughts to fly
Like hawks in the sky.

I had a dream a few weeks back (Friday, March 3rd, 2006). In it, a plane crashed into Marsabit Mountain because the distance had not been calculated correctly. As I ponder this meaning today, I am well aware of the fact that we must be very realistic in the difficult journey of the task ahead. Living in Northern Kenya is more than a hardship post. It is an isolated placement, far in distance, and demands a very challenging lifestyle. In all reality, we must be honest about the task ahead. Because Todd and I (and Corbi and Charese) have lived 15 years on the mission field, we might tend to lose our sensitivity on just how difficult this might be. Honest calculations are needed to ensure we make it safely.

And then the call is coupled with the intention of leading people on short-term missions, which requires sensitivity, compassion and the ability to look at life from their perspective.

I remember seeing my first giraffe on safari and going into the first Samburu hut and having chai with a bare-breasted woman with thousands of beads adorning her neck. I thought for sure she had been on the front cover of *National Geographic*. But as the journey goes on, I am rarely excited to have another cup of sour milk or another plate of ugali! But then I must remember that I am a guest in God's world. In the west, we have so many choices...what to eat, where to go, what transportation to take, what to wear, what kind of hobbies to partake in, what entertainment to watch...choices. But it's not that way everywhere in the world. Many countries don't offer freedom and choices in everyday life.

Lord, help me to be sensitive to the mission groups coming. In Rick Warren's book, *The Purpose Driven Church*, he explains that for a church to grow and reach out, its leaders must think like a non-believer. I think the same principle applies to missions. We see a main purpose of our ministry is to reach out to the non-missionary. We call it a "vacation with a purpose" targeted for individuals who might not otherwise have an opportunity to come to Africa and go on safari/mission. Thus, in order for us to be effective, we must begin to think like a non-missionary. This is a challenge for someone who has been on the field for so long and who has needed to THINK like a missionary in order to survive on the field. Bush living is not easy. After all, camping might be nice for a weekend when we want a simple lifestyle and some time sleeping under the stars. But to do this

24/7 – 365 days of the year will take a lot of preparation, hard work and planning!

LESSONS LEARNED ALONG THE DETOUR:

I cannot control my circumstances, but I can control my thinking, my attitude and my perspective on the situation. Reflective thinking enhances our assessment of the situation. When God brings me to a difficult place, I trust Him to sustain me while I engage in reflective thinking about the situation. Living a life that matters doesn't happen by chance. It happens by choice.

DETOUR PRAYER:

Lord, as I progress in this journey of life, help me to think differently. I want to succeed where I have failed before and go to a level I never dreamed possible. I want to become the person You want me to be. Help me change my thinking so that I may live into the calling You have placed upon my life. (Eph. 4:1) In Jesus' Name I pray. Amen

CHAPTER SIX

THE COST OF COMMITMENT

"When it comes time to die, make sure all you have
to do is die." Jim Elliot

*****

PREMONITION

Friday, March 3rd, 2006
St. Julian's Centre, Redhill, Kenya

My bedcovers jerked at 6:30 a.m. I awoke with a dream
about a plane crash.

*We were coming back from Marsabit on a small plane. Somehow
the calculation must have been wrong on how far it was because the plane
ran out of gas and crashed in a town, just a few feet from the airstrip.*

No one was hurt.

I felt the peace of the Lord through the whole thing. It was difficult for one teenage girl to process and after the accident she came out of her room to talk to her mom – also a short termer. "Short-term missions are hard enough." I explained to her and rubbed her back as she lay on the couch, "and now this plane crash. Give yourself time."

"But you had a dream this was coming," she said. "I've had many dreams", I said. "Some of them come true. I never can tell."

I read this in the Word just shortly after my dream. Isaiah 61:1-9 "The spirit of the Lord is upon me, because the Lord has appointed me to bring good news to the poor. He has sent me to comfort the brokenhearted and to announce that captives will be released and prisoners will be freed. He has sent me to tell those who mourn that the time of the Lord's favor has come and with it, the day of God's anger against the enemies. To all who mourn in Israel, he will give beauty for ashes, joy instead of mourning, praise instead of despair. For the Lord has planted them like strong and graceful oaks for his own glory…You will be called priests of the Lord, ministers of our God…instead of shame and dishonor, you will inherit a double portion of prosperity and everlasting joy".

*****

Approximately six weeks later, there was a fatal plane crash into Marsabit Mountain. We urgently requested the prayers of our family and friends through an email sent on Saturday, April 21st, 2006.

"It is most difficult to express our deep sadness of the sudden loss of our good friend and co-worker, The Rt. Rev. William Waqo, Provincial secretary of the Anglican Church of Kenya and Assistant Bishop of the Diocese of Kirinyaga. Yesterday, Bishop Waqo, along with six Members of Parliament and other government officials, died when the government Air Force plane crashed into Marsabit Mountain in bad weather. 18 people were flying to Marsabit, Northern Kenya, for a Peace Mission. Fifteen people died and the three survivors, including two crew members, remain in critical condition.

Bishop Waqo was on the Board of Directors for St. Julian's Centre, where the Rev. Patsy is the Manager. He was the person who recruited Todd to work in Northern Kenya among the unreached people groups. Todd and Patsy just traveled with Bishop Waqo in Northern Kenya for the commissioning of six evangelists three weeks ago. This Northern Region of Kenya has had fighting between the various ethnic groups for several years. Government officials traveling together were flying to the area for peace talks.

Please pray for the Anglican Church of Kenya and the country of Kenya, along with Bishop Waqo's wife, Naomi and their four children, Mary (15), Benson (10), Charis (2) (whose namesake is from our Charese) *and Tabitha (2 weeks old).*

*****

OUT OF THE BOX THINKING

Immediately after we heard the news of Bishop Waqo's death, several people gathered at the Anglican Church of Kenya Head Office in town, next to the ACK guesthouse. Adjacent to the guesthouse is the Bishop's residence in Nairobi. It was a good gathering place for people to meet, wait, talk, pray and make decisions. As we gathered, we shook hands, embraced and greeted one another. One woman shook my hand and said, "Bwana Asifiwe!," the Kiswahili equivalent to "Praise the Lord."

"Praise the Lord?" I questioned to myself. *Bishop Waqo is dead. How can we praise the Lord?* A small inner voice comforted me. *Yes, we praise the Lord, not because we are happy, but because He is still on the throne in all circumstances. He still remains Lord!*

Bishop Waqo, Todd and I had a superb working relationship. He was on the board of the Management Committee at St. Julian's Centre and was the key person who urged Todd to serve in Northern Kenya. We enjoyed brainstorming together. I remember our last trip together to Moyale, just four weeks prior to the accident. When discussing our dreams and vision for St. Julian's Centre and Northern Kenya, we said to each other, "Think out of the box." How can we do this strategically? How can we do this creatively? How can we do this realistically? In order that we would not get dragged into the same way of doing things time after time, we would say to one another, "Think out of the box!"

We thought out of the box when it came to fundraising and climbing Mt. Kilimanjaro. Certainly Bishop Waqo was thinking "out of the box" when he and a few others walked with a camel — in England – 80 kilometers from Cambridge to Oxford.

On the day following Bishop Waqo's death, we proceeded with family and supporting friends to receive his body as it was flown in with the other 13 who had died in the plane crash. It was a very somber event. President Kibaki was there, with his wife Lucy by his side, along with the vice President, former President Moi, several Members of Parliament and other dignitaries. Hundreds of people stood on the tarmac airstrip of Wilson airport as the military plane rolled down the runway. The Air Force band played Amazing Grace and 14 coffins were escorted off the plane, one at a time, with the Air Force soldiers marching in rhythm. I was in a daze and blankly stared at the coffins. Some had names, but most of the bodies, including Bishop Waqo's, remained unidentified. The coffins, wrapped in Kenyan flags, were carried by Air Force personnel and placed onto a table covered with white linen. As I gazed at the coffins, an inner voice said to me, "*Think out of the box. His body is no longer here. Think out of the coffin. Think out of the box.*"

This kind of thinking is the key to our relationship with Christ. It is the key to the cost of commitment. "For the message of the cross is foolishness to those who are perishing, but to us who are being saved it is the power of God."

"When Christ calls a man," says Dietrich Bonhoeffer, "he bids him come and die." There are different kinds of dying, it is true; but the essence of discipleship is contained in these words." The cost of commitment requires dying to the mediocrity of popular thinking.

Consider the cost of commitment – going against the flow of popular thinking. Bonhoeffer writes from prison, "Whenever it pleases God to put man into this world, the Christians must be ready for martyrdom and death. It is the only way that man learns faith."

Popular thinking says: "Save your life."
Christ says: "Lose your life."

Popular thinking says: "Take care of your own needs."
Christ says: "Give your life as a living sacrifice."

Popular thinking says: (and I am considering Bonhoeffer here) "Get out of prison at all costs, escape torture, and escape death." Bonhoeffer chose to remain in prison in order not to endanger others who might help him escape.

Think out of the box. Go against the flow of popular thinking. Think out of the coffin. Think beyond the grave. "Look not at the things which are seen, but at the things which are unseen: for the things which are seen are temporal, but the things that are unseen are eternal."

"For the message of the cross is foolishness to those who are perishing, but to those who are being saved, it is the power of God." Let us live in that power.

TAKE UP YOUR CROSS AND FOLLOW ME

Thursday, April 13th 2006

Here I am in Marsabit. We flew up yesterday for the burial of the late Bishop Waqo. Since we had to come as light as possible, I only brought my handbag, knowing that there were clothing and toiletries here. I only brought this small notebook to write in and my Bible; ironically, it is both of these that I do not want to face.

Where was God when it happened? Still on His throne, embracing this mighty man in His everlasting arms. The Bishop is now at His feet, praising His Savior. Someday, we will all understand. But today we just trust that there is a beautiful rainbow just beyond this big, black, storm cloud.

Where do my thoughts begin? To separate myself from the pain, I begin with the facts. I'll leave most of that to the reporters, journalist and paper coverage. After all, Bishop Waqo died an honorable death. President Kibaki, the First Lady, several Members of Parliament and the upcoming Uhuru Kenyatta were all present at yesterday's memorial service in the stadium. Planes flew in and out of the small Marsabit airstrip like this was an international airport. Military planes, missionary planes, private jets flew into Shegel because once again, the weather was too cloudy in Marsabit. Our plane, however, the deluxe "Menace in the Clouds," flew right into Marsabit. We were able to view the crash site. What a terrible death.

We have heard first hand reports that there were several people trapped inside the plane, calling for help on cell phones and screaming to people outside the plane to come to their rescue. But before they could assist, the plane burst into flames. Bishop Waqo's body was unidentifiable with the exception of his Seiko watch on his wrist and a small piece of cloth on his charred body.

Finally, I was able to dress myself this morning and just start walking one step at a time. That was after the chai and biscuit – which helped to give me strength as I have not eaten much in the past 3 days. I decided to take a soccer ball and a stuffed animal (bunny) over to the Waqo children. Because the only shoes brought from home were very uncomfortable, I searched through the used clothing donated by past short-term missioners and pulled out a fairly comfortable pair of sandals. I hadn't even arrived at the Waqo house before both heels fell off. I chuckled to myself and got there without too many stones in my foot. When I arrived at the Waqo house, the house and yard were filled with over a hundred people. The Borana culture declares three days of constant visitation by friends and family – the widowed family provides all their meals. People travel long distances and sleep in the house, cramping the hallway, outside and even sleeping on the floor in the same room as the widow.

When I went to see Naomi this morning, women were wailing as they expressed their sadness, and some were fainting at her feet. When I got to the house and greeted Naomi she asked if I could take the children home with me and they could stay at my house. I was so grateful to be able to do something practical. People want to help, but many times we don't know what to do. So, Benson, Mary and Charis came back with me, ate lunch with Todd joining us, and now they have been resting for almost two hours. I dug out pencils, pencil sharpener, coloring book and crayons and Bible quip book, again from the duffle bag the last missioners left behind. Amazing how all that give-away stuff has come in very handy.

We're coming back again on Tuesday. It has been very good that I have come; I can understand why I was one who got on the plane as they chose very carefully who would go. They only had seats for a few. Being here to support Rev. Naomi and the family has allowed us to help care for the children, along with host Archbishop Nzimbi, his wife, Alice and Bishop Daniel.

The Lord does not take long to use the gifts and talents consecrated to Him. Just a week ago today we dedicated this house to the Lord with a small house warming reception with the staff and evangelists. Ever since that night the Lord has been using this house to glorify Him, and tonight, Benson, Mary and Charis sleep together in the guest bedroom.

Yesterday, as we buried Bishop Waqo's body and put it into the grave, the crowd was pushing and I found myself directly behind the casket. At the same time, Todd was in front of the casket, carrying the cross. It was a moving analogy, almost a prophetic word picture. Take up your cross and follow me. With Jesus at the forefront, Todd will lead, and carry the cross. I will follow. To God be the glory.

*****

WEDDING RING

Three days after the plane crashed into Marsabit Mountain, an elderly man walked into Naomi's home in Marsabit. Although she had never seen him before, the man walked right up to Naomi and presented into her palm, a gift. It was her husband's wedding ring. Only slightly charred by the flames, the name engraved on the inside of the gold band was still very readable. N-A-O-M-I. And the date of their wedding, almost 17 years ago.

"Patsy," Naomi explained to me. "This ring has stopped me crying. It has been very hard for me to accept my husband's death because I could not identify his face. But this, this is something I can hold on to. This was my husband's way of saying goodbye."

Only a few weeks before the accident, Naomi and Bishop Waqo had enlarged their rings because they were too difficult to remove. Now that very ring had become tangible evidence that her husband thought of her until the end, when he finally slipped it off his finger, threw it out of the flames far enough so that it would not melt as his Bishop's ring did, but found and returned, to the one he most loved on earth.

"I believe he prayed, Patsy." Naomi continued her story. "I believe he prayed that this ring would be found, and brought to me."

*****

MY WEDDING RING STORY

For those of you who have read my first book, *A Guest in God's World: Memories of Madagascar*, you would have read about the loss of my wedding ring on the day we flew out from the States to work in Madagascar in 1991. I counted this ring as lost forever. It was the final symbol of everything I had given to the Lord.

In the summer of 2008 my parents were refurbishing their bathroom. My mother was to be out of town when the plumber was scheduled to come, so she left him a note. *"When you take this sink apart, please look out for a small wedding band which slipped down the overflow hole."*

When she arrived home, stuck to her bathroom mirror was her note and my wedding band. After speaking to the plumber, he told my mother he was amazed the gold band had not slipped all the way down the pipe into the sewage system. It had been caught on a tiny snag and held there all these years.

My mother wrapped it a box and gave it to me at one of our customary table gift exchanges. I was awestruck and speechless (for once!). The most precious possession I had given up at the time was the final thing I had put on the altar of sacrifice. I had counted it as lost, but the Lord had not. He cared. He respected the desires of my heart.

He honored my sacrifice and brought the band back to me after 17 years.

A ring is a tangible possession of a sacred marriage between husband and wife. The significance of seeing my ring which had been held in place all these years brought comfort. I thought of Naomi who was also given back the precious symbol of love between husband and wife.

*****

PEACE BE WITH YOU
"Whatever you do, work at it with all your heart, as working for the Lord, not for men."
Bishop Waqo's life verse Col. 3:23

A few months later, I sat with Naomi Waqo, who was going back to Marsabit for the first time after her husband's death. On the plane, she shared these stories.

On Wednesday, June 14th, 2006, Naomi's sister, Sarah, called Naomi from Moyale, the northern border town of Ethiopia and Kenya. Sarah, who is not yet strong in her faith, told Naomi on the phone that while she was sleeping for one hour during the day, the late Bishop Waqo appeared to her. She wanted to hug him. But he spoke to her in her mother tongue of Borana, "No, No. This body is a holy body. I am no longer in the flesh. Where I am, I am very happy and you seem to be so much disturbed. Do not be disturbed anymore." (Peace with you.)

Then he continued, "Tell Mama Kule (Naomi) that when I have appeared to her, she has always been excited and laughing. But tell her she should not do that anymore for I am no longer in the flesh."

Then my sister asked him, "Have you been visiting her?" (Because Naomi had never shared with her about the Bishop's previous appearance to her.) "Yes!" the Bishop said. "And that is what she has been doing."

My sister called to give me the message. I told her, "How can I avoid being excited and laughing when I see him?" (What she meant by being excited and happy was as though he was still on earth living with them again.)

Even though Naomi has only shared this story with me and Rev. Kampicha (and she has given me permission to write about it) this is not the only person who has come to her with such an account. Actually, the first story came from one of the late Bishop Waqo's best friends. He was with Bishop Waqo the night before he died. This man, who was once a Christian and then became Muslim, came to Naomi several weeks ago and shared the following story.

"Last night I didn't sleep. When I went to bed, the Bishop came, stood in front of my bed. Speaking in Borana, the Bishop said to me, "If one is to work or do anything, one has to do as I have done.""

George Catache, whom the Bishop called Gollo, continued his story. "A second time he came to me on top of a mountain and showed me a very nice place, glittering....shining and full of many good things. The Bishop spoke to me and said, "Gollo, that is where I am". And then he left. When he shared this with his wife, she said, "He has shown you heaven.""

As Naomi and I flew over the edge of the Chelbe desert she gave her interpretation. "This could be about faith. They were friends. He was a Christian but changed to Muslim. In the dream my husband said, 'One has to do as I have done. My husband gave up his life for Christ. Why I believe this is because what he is saying in the dream is true."

Bishop Waqo has appeared to Naomi four times, during the night when she has been asleep. "The third time, I was sleeping at night and dreamt that we were at the cathedral together. We were all together – you, Todd, the Archbishop – several Christians. The bishop came and greeted everybody. Everybody was rejoicing; then someone went to get the Archbishop to tell him that the Bishop had returned because he was not aware of what was going on!"

At first, when these mysteries were happening to Rev. Naomi she thought she was still holding on to the memories of her husband. She thought she still had to give him up and release him to the Lord. But now she is beginning to understand. "This is not a psychological problem." She stated to me. "Oh, no," I answered her. "It's a spiritual awakening!"

When Jesus appeared to his disciples (Luke 24:35) he did two things. First of all, he brought comfort, "Peace be with you." Secondly, he appeared to them to strengthen their faith, "They were terribly frightened."

Naomi commented, "I am taking death differently than before. This confirms to me that this person is with us spiritually. I'm learning a lot and drawing closer to God, no longer doubting heaven."

*****

WHAT'S GOING TO HAPPEN TO ME WHEN I DIE?

When I (Patsy) was 16 years old, I went to my youth leader and asked him, *"What is going to happen to me when I die?"* With a cigarette in one hand and a beer in the other, he responded, "Good question, why don't you tell me?" This bizarre answer to my crucial question was probably the beginning of my spiritual awakening, and my quest for spiritual life and purpose on earth began during those teenage years.

A few months after the death of Bishop Waqo I was having lunch with Naomi, and we talked about life, death and life after death. We were discussing what it might be like when we get to heaven. Will we recognize those people on earth, which were so dear to us? Will we still be of service to the Lord or will we just sit as His feet, praising Him?! What will we be doing? Will we be able to view "earth" from below? Will we somehow know what is still going on?

Some questions are not meant to have answers this side of death. This is part of the mystery of faith. If mysteries were to be explained, they would not be called mysteries!

*****

AMBASSADORS FOR CHRIST

"We are therefore Christ's ambassadors, as though God were making his appeal through us. We implore you on Christ's behalf: Be reconciled to God." 2 Cor 5:20

Sermon Preached by Patsy
May/June 2006, St. Julian's Chapel

After Bishop Waqo's death, I decided I would preach a five part series on the "Cost of Commitment," taking thoughts from the book Bishop Waqo adamantly suggested Naomi read just days before his death. Here are excerpts from one of those sermons.

When looking up the definition of "ambassador", we find the following: a diplomat accredited to a foreign government or sovereign as a resident representative, or appointed for a special diplomatic assignment; or somebody who represents or promotes a quality.

In the thesaurus, synonyms include envoy, emissary, resident minister, diplomat, legation, mission, and negotiator.

This week, I was fortunate. Two representatives from the Swedish Embassy came for an overnight meeting and strategic planning at St. Julian's Centre, and I grabbed the opportunity and asked them their informal definitions of ambassador. They suggested the following definitions: the highest representative of one country to another; someone who represents the interests and policies of that country and gauges the situation in the host country, bringing both countries together; a spokesperson, one who enhances the relationship between the two countries, he/she is a facilitator of good relations.

It sounds very much like the late Bishop Waqo's words that I heard just six weeks ago today. On Sunday, March 19th, I took notes as he preached at a service in Moyale. When re-reading my journal this past week, I found the following, "The role of the church is not to speak here at the pulpit but to transform society in every realm – we are Ambassadors of Christ in all aspects of life. Initiate peace and reconciliation – especially here in Northern Kenya."

As it says in the *Expositor's Bible Commentary* for 2 Cor. 5:20 "We are therefore Christ's ambassadors, as though God were making his appeal through us. We implore you on Christ's behalf: Be reconciled to God." Reconciliation is not some polite ignoring or reduction of hostility but rather it is total and objective removal. Bishop Waqo fought until the end to bring peace and reconciliation to the nation of Kenya.

I believe it was this benefit of true peace and reconciliation that the Lord brought to the people in that plane crash just three weeks ago. Bishop Waqo was on that plane for a reason. He was a purpose-driven man who loved the Lord dearly and lived with the end in mind. He was a true Ambassador for Christ who transformed society in every realm. His life was a living testimony. Growing up as a Muslim, he discovered the transforming resurrection power of the Lord Jesus Christ in secondary school, and it was his true vision to proclaim this power throughout the universe.

He has done just that. Even at the memorial service at All Saints on Friday, April 21st, a journalist from The Nation was moved to tears and gave her life to the Lord. During the service she was transformed, reconciled to God and traded her Muslim belief for a decision for Christ.

Since the plane crash on April 10th, it has been a blessing for Naomi and me to talk and discuss the ways that the Lord seems to have been preparing many for the actual event itself.

It was interesting for me to go back to the dream I had six weeks ago. When I did, I questioned the Lord. "But Lord, in my dream, no one was hurt. Why in this plane crash were several people killed?" Then the quiet voice within me came again. "15 people were killed; no one was hurt. No *souls* were hurt."

Our transient life is not what it seems. It is much shorter than we can ever anticipate. I believe Bishop Waqo preached to the end and brought a message of greater peace and reconciliation to those on the plane: Muslims, Christians, various ethnic groups, enemies of one another, fist-fighting before they even got on the plane that morning. But in their last moments they had 10 minutes to make a decision for Christ. For a greater cause, God allowed them *not* to die instantly in the crash, but to have time to be reconciled to God through the fire. As the plane went up in flames, a witness told the family, Bishop Waqo's voice was heard proclaiming 'My God, My God, My God.'

God gave us the ministry of reconciliation. God is not counting men's sins against them and has committed to us the message of reconciliation. We are therefore Christ's ambassadors, as though God were making his appeal through us. We implore you on Christ's behalf: Be reconciled to God. For he says, "In the time of my favor I heard you and in the day of salvation I helped you." I tell you, now is the time of God's favor, now is the day of salvation.

*****

THE LARGE, BLACK SACK

Certainly Naomi did not choose this detour of her husband's death to interrupt the plans for her life. But had the Lord prepared her in some way? Three years ago when the late Bishop Waqo was consecrated as bishop, Naomi had a premonition. During the service, when the Archbishop and bishops were laying hands on Naomi and her husband, Naomi envisioned herself carrying a very large, black sack. The spirit was upon her, and she was moved to tears. People around her thought they were tears of happiness; however, she knew herself that the sack would be very heavy, and for her, at that moment, hers were tears of sacrifice – considering the cost of commitment.

After Bishop Waqo's funeral service in Marsabit, Naomi testified that the Lord had prepared her for her husband's death as she recalled the premonition she had had on the day of Bishop Waqo's consecration – the vision of herself carrying that very large, black sack upon her back.

A day before his death, Bishop Waqo gave his wife a book called, *The Cost of Commitment*, stating emphatically, "Read this from cover to cover." I decided to examine it myself, grappling for insight into what Bishop Waqo must have been thinking. While reading the book, I prayed about Naomi's premonition. The psalmist writes in Ps. 126:5-6, "Those who sow in tears will reap with songs of joy. He who goes out weeping, carrying seed to sow, will return with songs of joy, carrying sheaves with him."

Couldn't that be the paradox of life from death? Couldn't the black sack actually be a sack of grain, for "unless a kernel of wheat falls to the ground and dies, it remains only a single seed. But if it dies, it produces many seeds. The man who loves his life will lose it, while the man who hates his life in this world will keep it for eternal life." (John 12:24-25)

Yes, the Lord had given Naomi a large sack to carry. But does He not work out all things for good for those who love the Lord and for those He has called according to His purpose? (Rom. 8:28) Can the hour of actual death be the hour for the Son of Man to be glorified? Death actually means the beginning of eternal life. "The man who loves his life will lose it, while the man who hates his life in this world will keep it for eternal life." (John 12:25) By facing death one starts to live. The paradox is real. As Bonhoeffer says, "When Jesus Christ calls a man he bids him come and die."

*****

A WISE WOMAN'S WORDS

In service to the Lord and ministry, not only do the men have to consider the cost of commitment, but their wives as well. Elisabeth Elliot writes: "The other wives and I talked together one night about the possibility of becoming widows.

Each of us knew when we married our husbands that there would never be any question about who came first – God and His work held first place in each life. It was the condition of true discipleship; it became devastatingly meaningful now."

*****

"IF YOU WANT TO GO FAR, GO TOGETHER. IF YOU WANT TO GO FAST, GO ALONE."
African Proverb

On our last trip together to Marsabit and Moyale, Bishop Waqo told me an African proverb, "If you want to go far," he said, "go together. If you want to go fast, go alone."

We are not in this faith journey by ourselves! Remember, as the Africans say, "We are together!" "I am because we are!" (John Mbiti)

We are the body of Christ – the community of faith, surrounded by so great a cloud of witnesses. "Therefore, let us throw off everything that hinders and the sin that so easily entangles, and let us run with perseverance the race marked out for us."

LESSONS LEARNED ALONG THE DETOUR:

Jesus wept.

DETOUR PRAYER:

Dear Lord, help me through this pain. In Jesus' Name, Amen.

CHAPTER SEVEN

I AM BECAUSE WE ARE

A person is a person through other persons.

- African Proverb

Since I had become Manager of St. Julian's Centre, I had been learning about relationships; staff unity, living in community, family dynamics. "We all live public lives; our relationship with Christ is constantly on display before a watching, watch-me world."[xi] Our witness to the staff is a daily exercise and holds us accountable to one another and to God.

We all need deep friendships and people who will see us for who we are: weak, incomplete, a mere portion of who God designed us to be. In these relationships we are able to go beyond the public image. We are able to reveal ourselves to people who are not impressed by our gifts, who maybe have never even seen those gifts in use. These trusted friends dare us to go deeper and help us sort out lies from reality. They challenge us to be discontent with anything less than a rich life with God and through God, a life that transforms the world.[xii]

I believe that family can bring us into balance and wholeness, proving whether our solitude and times with the Lord really change us. Without relationships, who challenges our spirituality and integrity? We need people who will see our weakness, love us in spite of them and ask us the tough questions. "What will be different now? What will you change about the way you live?" Loved ones like this challenge us to grow and risk relationally.

"Small groups break through the 'we don't need relationships' myth and invite us into community, vulnerability and acceptance. They challenge us beyond 'that's just the way I am' living. Families and roommates are privy to disparity between our stage and dressing room, and we can free them to ask hard questions. In solitude we sit with those questions, viewing family as part of the refining process God uses to eliminate the fool's gold from the pan of our life."[xiii]

This is what I desire in my relationships with my closest friends and family members. I thank God that I have the ability and openness to talk heart to heart with my husband and daughters. I thank God that we realize each one has limitations and weaknesses but that through the grace of God we will someday become all He intends us to be. And we are to help each other along the journey, challenging them to grow deeper in Christ and with each other. I also thank God that I have this challenging relationship with a few dear friends. "Friends who are committed to our wholeness likewise call us lovingly into growth."[xiv] I am thankful for the friendships we have drawn upon here in Kenya. Everywhere God has taken us He has provided a few close friends. This has been an on-going prayer request and He has answered it every step of the way.

These friends challenge me, causing me to be all I am in Christ. They love me for who I am – strengths and weaknesses combined – and in the end they are my biggest cheerleaders. When I am running the race of life, I see their faces towards the finish line, cheering me on with their loudest voice, for they know how much I struggled to get there and they celebrate the victory with me when I am finished. Like our team climbing Mt. Kilimanjaro, our group struggled to get up the mountain and celebrated together at the end.

David Benner, in his book *Spiritual Companions,* confronts the reader with ideals of spiritual friendship.

"If you are blessed to have one or more genuine spiritual friendships, be sure to thank God, because such friendships are not an entitlement but a gift. Christ, who said to his disciples, "You have not chosen me, but I have chosen you," might say of Christian friends, "You have not chosen each other, but I have chosen you for each other. Spiritual friendship is not a reward for good behavior. It is the means by which God reveals his goodness by helping us know others and ourselves and thereby know him. It is a gift God gives to us. It is a gift we can give to others."[xv]

Lord, help me to truly appreciate the friends I have, cultivating their relationships like a farmer would a precious crop. As I sow these seeds of friendship and intimacy, may I reap a great harvest.

*****

GOD TAKES THE WHOLE PACKAGE

May 17th, 2006
St. Julian's Centre, Redhill, Kenya
In bed with bronchitis

One of my spiritual mentors is Elisabeth Elliot. She has first influenced me through her Christian literature, and secondly by a visit she made to Madagascar in January 2000. At my invitation, although I had never met Elisabeth, she allotted time from her busy schedule to travel almost halfway around the world to visit us in Madagascar. For one week in Madagascar, Elisabeth and her husband, Lars Gren, lived with us, ministered to the Malagasy people and spoke to fellow missionaries. In our leisure hours at home, Elisabeth told jokes, played the piano and cut Corbi's hair, all the while sharing stories of her missionary life in Ecuador. When we came back to the USA on our next furlough, Elisabeth and Lars invited us to their home on Strawberry Cove. It was there that I saw original black and white photos of her and Valerie, living among the Aucas, even sleeping in hammocks at night. Getting a glass of water for myself in their kitchen, I glanced at quotes held by refrigerator magnets that I had previously read in her books. Among my priceless possessions today are the autographed books she gave me during her stay – not only her own writings, but also one of Amy Carmichael's as she was Elisabeth's mentor.

One night she told us the story of the five young martyrs of faith who dared to make contact with the Auca Indians. One of these men was her first husband. Even after his death, she continued to live in the area with the men who murdered her husband. To me, this is the ultimate faith. Elisabeth Elliot doesn't see it this way. She writes the following in her book, *Through the Gates of Splendor*, penned at her home in Magnolia, Massachusetts.

"It is not the level of our spirituality that we can depend on. It is God and nothing less than God, for the work is God, and the call is God and everything is summoned by Him and to His purposes, the whole scene, the whole mess, the whole package – our bravery and our cowardice, our love and our selfishness, our strengths and our weaknesses. God can take a murderer like

Moses, an adulterer like David and a traitor like Peter and make of them strong servants of His."[xvi]

Elisabeth writes, "I think back to the five men themselves, remembering Pete's agony of indecision as to whether he should join the others in the venture, Ed's eagerness to go even though Marylou was eight months pregnant, his strong assurance that all would be well, Roj's depression and deep sense of failure as a missionary, Nate's extreme caution and determination, Jim's nearly reckless exuberance."[xvii]

These words give me great comfort in my view of myself as a missionary: eleven years in Madagascar and now three in Kenya. God uses all of us. Todd seems to be full of enthusiasm, willing to walk forward and break new ground. I, on the other hand, tend to compare my ministry with my husband's and become doubtful of whether I am really making a difference as a missionary! Thank God that He sees beyond our worthless selves and uses even the least of us who are made precious in His sight and in His image.

*****

WHAT DOES IT TAKE TO BE A MISSIONARY?
LOVE PEOPLE.

May 18th, 2006
St. Julian's Centre, Redhill, Kenya

Maybe we overemphasize the "call" of a missionary life. To throw away Jim Elliot's life among ignorant savages was thought "absurd."[xviii] But these missionaries wanted to obey God. Pete Fleming wrote to his fiancée, Olive Ainslie. "I think a 'call' to the mission field is no different from any other means of guidance. A call is nothing more or less than obedience to the will of God, as God presses it home to the soul by whatever means He chooses."[xix]

Jim Elliot writes in his diary about his call into missions. "My going to Ecuador is God's counsel, as is my leaving Betty and my refusal to be counseled by all who insist I should stay and stir up believers in the U.S. And how do I know it is His counsel? 'Yes, my heart instructed me in the night seasons.' Oh, how good! For I have known my heart is speaking to me for God! No visions, no voices, but the counsel of a heart which desires God."[xx]

Maybe a missionaries "calling" is rather a responsibility to cross cultural boundaries and love our neighbor as ourselves. Pete Fleming's first thoughts when seeing the first Indians in Ecuador was, 'Yes, I can love these people.'[xxi] We are challenged to do the same. Love people.

Teamwork, strategic planning and a love for God and fellow human beings will help us cross cultural boundaries and love this world for Christ. The missionaries had gone to Ecuador to reach the Quichuas with the Word of God, a task for which they were prepared but could accomplish only if they gained the Quichua's confidence and love. By living among them, sharing in their lives and laying the foundations of mutual trust they hoped to open the minds and hearts of the Indians to the Christian message.[xxii] Truly this is an example of the Great Commission being lived out through the Great Commandment - loving our neighbors as ourselves.

*****

INFINITE ADAPTABILITY

May 19th, 2009
St. Julian's Centre, Rehill, Kenya

I have all this time to ponder my thoughts as I am still in bed with bronchitis. I continue to read the words of Elisabeth Elliot.

> "The life of a missionary calls for infinite adaptability
> – from winning a national oratorical contest to strug-
> gling with an unwritten language…from starring on
> the college football field to teaching a bunch of small

Indians to play volleyball...from prospects of a law career in a North American city to a life in the jungle of South America. Marylou, who had been director of music in a large church, slowly and carefully taught Indian children to sing two-line songs which she and Ed had written in the Quichua language."[xxiii] Missionaries must be 1) infinitely adaptable, 2) constantly face expendability and 3) be extremely creative.

"Soldiers (go) into battle, knowing the price they might have to pay for their country. Yet when the Lord Jesus asks us to pay the price for world evangelization, we often answer without a word. We cannot go. We say it costs too much."[xxiv] "Obedience is not a momentary option; it is a die cast decision made beforehand."[xxv] In other words, "Wherever you are, *be all there*. Live to the hilt every situation you believe to be the will of God."[xxvi]

Some missionaries just go off on their own. But if we do this, where is the sense of community? What about the biblical example of going out in pairs and the use of the kinship of believers, the Church? Or, do some missionaries rebel against the Church, the body of Christ and strike out on their own? Is the mission field an escape for some?

Many questions, fewer answers. Lord, help us to find insight and search for the answers to the questions above. Give us accountability within the body of Christ and spiritual companions and mentors along the way.

*****

LESSONS LEARNED ALONG THE DETOUR:

We do not need to make the journey alone. This is God's purpose for creating us together in community as the body of Christ, knitting us together so each part does its work. (Eph. 4:16) The church is a family. It has a responsibility to provide a safe place in which we can create authentic and significant relationships based on grace, love, acceptance and integrity.

DETOUR PRAYER:

Thank You, Lord, that under Your direction, the whole body of Christ is fitted together perfectly. As each part does its own special work, help us to facilitate the other parts to grow, so that the whole body is healthy and growing and full of love. (Eph. 4:16) May we take responsibility in playing our role in the body of Christ and to lead a life worthy of our calling, (Eph. 4:1) equipping God's people to do His work and build up the church, the body of Christ, until we come to such unity in our faith and knowledge of God's Son that we will be mature and full grown in the Lord, measuring up to the full stature of Christ. (Eph. 4:12-13). Thank you, Lord, for the saints who have gone before us and have shown us the way.

CHAPTER EIGHT

PEOPLE REACHING PEOPLE

Tell me – I'll forget

Show me – I may remember

Involve me – I'll understand

- Mike

*****

WHEN? WHERE?

"I always wanted to do something like that!"

Some people are excited about the idea when I encourage them to come and experience first hand what God is doing in Africa. Other times I find resistance. Perhaps they think going on a short-term mission might be part of their own detour and fight the idea like I did my missionary service for several years! Instead of explaining missionary life as a "calling" I prefer to explain it as a "responsibility" to live out the Great Commandment (To love the Lord our God with all our hearts, souls and minds and our neighbor as ourselves) through the Great Commission (Go and make disciples of all nations.)

The question people need to ask themselves should no longer be: 'Do I have enough money?' or 'Can I get enough vacation time?' but 'When do I go?' and 'Where?'

"Short-term missions are the most exciting development in recent mission's history. Missions are no longer just a faraway concept, but a very real and personal commitment. God's people are rising up like never before to go to the ends of the earth."[xxvii]

There is no doubt that the local hosting church, the individual missioner and the receiving church all benefit from their partnership in the gospel. "Church-to-Church partnership most often releases awakening and revival into a church, releasing people for witness at home and abroad."[xxviii]

*****

A PILGRIMAGE

Comments on a Pilgrimage to Kenya, Fall 2004, By: R. Scott Purdy, Vestryman

A wise and wealthy philanthropist once told me that charity was one of the hardest things to do. He went on to clarify that he did not mean the act of generosity was difficult – the difficulty lay in making sure your donations were channeled toward the intended work, and not diverted to less lofty use. He also taught that one could make small donations to each charity that asked – and ultimately make no meaningful impact to any of them, nor any of their causes – or carefully choose a small handful of charities, provide significant continuing support to these, and produce a consequential influence through their enhanced work.

Many question the benefit of short-term mission trips. Is any good really being done? Isn't this really a vacation for those going? Wouldn't more benefit be gained by just sending the money instead of sending people – who will just "get in the way?"

Yet a key benefit of a short-term mission (in addition to the enhancement of bonds through fellowship) is the opportunity to see first-hand whether your continued financial support is warranted by the stewardship and outreach practices of the ministry "on the ground." Short-term visitation is a critical component in choosing which ministries to support.

It gives you a chance to see the following:

- the needs
- who is being helped
- how the help is provided
- if the help is efficient and effective
- if money is carefully stewarded
- if the intent of the ministry matches your own

I am in the final days of a short-term mission trip in east Africa. We have witnessed the poles of the spectrum of effective ministries. One which was overwhelmingly positive and clearly saving souls (The McGregor's) – another which is probably best described simply as the "Contrary."

A brief description of our pilgrimage may assist others in their expectations, should they contemplate a similar visit.

Week 1:

We arrived late Saturday, and stayed at St. Julian's Centre in Limuru near Nairobi (which the McGregor's manage on behalf of the Anglican Church of Kenya [the "ACK"]). We worshipped at a nearby church Sunday morning and immediately went out to Nakuru National Park. In our 24 hours in Nakuru we saw: over 30 rhinos, two leopards, tens of thousands of flamingos, hundreds of pink pelicans and dozens of storks; Cape buffalo, hundreds of zebras, dozens of giraffe, baboons, hyenas, and many other animals.

Tuesday we flew north to Marsabit, and the desert regions of Kenya to visit the "unreached" peoples of the desert tribes. We witnessed the work of Todd and Patsy McGregor in spreading the Gospel to these people. We saw Samburu warriors in their colorful daily garb and went inside huts and discussed creation with the elders of the Gabbra tribe underneath "the tree" in the desert. We visited schools where boys sleep 120 in a small dorm room. We saw a string of 40 camels and prayed over the sick and the dying. We flew in a small Cessna and landed on a dirt airstrip in the desert.

Week 2:

We arrived back at St. Julian's Tuesday afternoon, and had dinner with the other guests – who were attending a training conference for their ministry. St. Julian's is a hub meeting point for many ministries throughout East Africa.

Wednesday Fr. Mark & I toured bits of Nairobi with Patsy McGregor and her daughters, Corbi and Charese. Fr. Mark and I met with Dr. Esther Mombo, the Academic Dean of St. Paul's United Theological Seminary in Limuru. We had an open and informative discussion about the status of the Anglican Communion.

We have seen His wondrous works in animals, people, and ministry. We thank God for the ministry of the McGregor's and encourage others to witness it and to experience its encouragement.

We praise God for His works! We thank Him for the gift of our salvation through His Son our Savior Jesus Christ! We raise all our hopes to the risen Christ!

*****

WHAT ARE WE GOING TO DO?
By Charese McGregor

One of the most common questions we are asked by short term mission teams is "What are we going to DO?" With the emphasis on DO! Our response? "Can you hug babies?

Can you hold somebody's hand?" Can we reach out to be people reaching people?! Here is Charese's perspective:

Driving down the bumpy, dusty road, I used body language to communicate with the local Samburu people. With a native translator alongside in the truck, my family drove on the edge of the Chelbi Desert. Driving towards our destination we see Samburu warriors who, we are told, killed a lion a few days earlier. As we approached the site, I glanced through red, dust covered windows to see the hosting community gathered, singing songs of welcome.

Stepping outside into the African culture, I was awestruck as women thanked me for coming to build a church. I exchanged bracelets with a young woman - mine a pink plastic one, worn to fight against breast cancer, and hers a handmade beaded one. Then together, we continued our work.

Over the next week, I visited the woman daily. Through this experience, I was able to set my priorities straight by building relationships first rather than always being focused on doing something, such as constructing the church.

*****

LANE'S RULES FOR MISSIONERS

Stuart Lane was a missionary with the Episcopal Church, serving in Malawi for several years. Through his wisdom and experience, he wrote the following suggestions for missioners.

1. Listen more than you talk.
2. Learn more than you teach.
3. Submit more than you rule.
4. Give more honor and respect than you accept.
5. Spend more on wages than on goods.
6. Spend more on local goods than imported ones.
7. Concentrate on loving people rather than on doing good.
8. Build relationships instead of monuments.
9. Always assume that your hosts have good reasons for what they do.
10. Never condemn behavior until you understand why it occurs.

*****

THE STENCH OF DEATH

June 2006

St. Julian's Centre, Redhill, Kenya

Todd called last night after three days of no communication because his phone battery was used up and he had no way of recharging – he was out on site for the mission team and came into Marsabit to shower and get proper rest before today's baptismal service. He sounded like a little kid in a candy shop – happy, light hearted, joyous in the Lord and what He is doing in the North. They have had a fantastic response to the Gospel and are expecting to baptize between 40 and 50 today. There is even hint of someone donating property to build a secondary school – Praise the Lord!

He was overjoyed and amazed that a local villager walked 25 km to Marsabit to tell the Member of Parliament what a great work went on with the medical mission. What a blessing to have short-term teams come and minister!

Amidst the joy, however, Todd was also aware of the physical suffering that still remained a reality for the people. The facts could not be denied: 17 people were dying daily because of the famine. As Todd stated, "It was the first time that I have experienced smelling the stench of death."

*****

TESTIMONY

A group of 13 University students from the United Kingdom, led by James Griffin, came to Northern Kenya and organized a soccer tournament. "Taking part in a mission team will strengthen your faith, touch your heart, deepen your friendships and change your life."[xxix] Here is a collection of emails from some of those team members transformed by their experience in Africa.

17th August 2006

Even though this is only our third day here in Marsabit, so much has happened. We flew here on Tuesday morning from Nairobi on planes so small that we needed to weigh ourselves as well as our luggage to ensure that we had enough fuel on board to get us here safely! It was so amazing to see the beautiful landscape, with a particular highlight being the view of Mt. Kenya from the air. We have since been in frequent contact with Todd, the missionary here in Marsabit, who has been a great help to us, especially in telling us the peculiarities of each tribe and ensuring that our preaching is culturally sensitive.

Marsabit is, obviously, very different from back home. Even though Marsabit is on lots of world maps, it does strike you as being very small and rural enough for it to be totally normal for goats and cattle to roam up and down the main street of the town (showing absolutely no fear toward the vehicles)!

In the centre of town, the "mzungu" (white foreigners) have become minor celebrities, and even when we've just been standing in shops, often a group of approximately ten will just stand around to have a look at us! It has been noticed that the flushing toilets we've been used to at home have been replaced for holes in the ground...In spite of that, we've been so struck by the warmth of the people here and the way in which we've been made to feel so welcome.

We are going into the second day of our first school visit at Manyatta Jillo School. The first day was encouraging even though many of us were daunted by the thought of the language barrier and the unfamiliarity of the Kenya classroom – where the stick and learning-by-rote are the order of the day. The kids were really very responsive, bearing in mind the gulf in experience between our two cultures, and they really did warm to us, which was such a response to prayer. They have had a lot of fun with the footballs (American soccer balls) that we've brought as they'd been playing football with rolled up plastic bags tied together with string. The older people in the community seem to be very appreciative of what we are doing in the schools as well, which is a real plus.

*****

KAMBOE: A PICTURE POSTCARD

24th August, 2006

The team has just come back from our mission in Kamboe, which was about a two hour truck drive from Marsabit. It seems that in this part of the world you are far more likely to be clinging onto the side of a truck than actually sitting inside it when going from one place to another! So after sharing transport with goats, chickens, water tanks and 38 other people, we got out of the truck and started the mission.

The mission at Kamboe was a totally new experience for us. It is really quite remote, and was in many ways quite a "picture postcard" tribal village – almost all of the inhabitants wear traditional Samburu tribal dress, the people live in huts made out of sticks and cow dung, and the village elders assemble under the acacia trees every afternoon to sleep and make important decisions related to the town.

There had actually been a medical mission to Kamboe in June, led by Rev. Todd, which had an amazing response, with around 200 people (30% of the village) coming to faith in a week. Our main aim was to try and encourage and deepen the faith of the new believers and also to try and share the good News with those that hadn't heard before. In the mornings we went around the huts with a translator, introducing ourselves, meeting the villagers and sharing Scripture. Unlike in the UK, everyone was interested in what we had to say! In the afternoons we had more structured teaching with the different groups of the village – the elders, the married women, the youth and the children, while in the evenings we had a celebration open to everyone that had lots of praise and a sermon.

There was real evidence of God preparing the way for us and even working through us. We were amazed at how willing these people were to receive teaching, to the point that even when there was a conflict involving men that had raided the elders' cattle and the police; they still wanted to hear our preaching before dealing with the incident. We were particularly encouraged at how the elders received our message, with one of them even donating some of his land for free so that a church could be built next to the focal point of the village – the elders' tree. We were also told that the community particularly valued the fact that we had involved everyone in the village with our mission, including the woman and children, and not just focused on the elders.

Some of us found that we took to Kamboe like a duck to water – it has been a running joke that Sanjay enjoyed his time so much that it is a miracle that he got on the truck home instead of undergoing the necessary adult circumcision. However, the real threat of scorpion bites (as Todd has experienced first hand) led nine of us to sleep in the truck on 3 single mattresses, which meant that a good proportion of the team got an incredible view of the stars, but not a very good night's sleep. This was not helped by some of the Kenyan contingent on the mission team starting an impromptu worship session at 5am!

*****

BUBISA – TOWN OF THE WIND

August 2006

We finished our time in the schools in Bubisa, a town about an hour away that is populated by the Gabbra tribe. Bubisa was physically very different to the other places that we have been to. It was in the middle of a desert, and very windy – its name means windy in the local language.

We have moved on to the most intense part of the mission – the football/soccer tournament. It has been encouraging to see how much the local community has supported the tournament, with around 2,000 people at the pitch on the first day. The logistics have gone well. A generator was found just at the right time to broadcast the game and announcements.

Our first match ended with a 2-1 loss. We feel like we played fairly well and were able to keep a good Christian witness.

*****

KCB SPONSORS PEACE TOURNAMENT

The short-term missions group transformed society as well, seeking to bringing peace to a disturbed region. Here is a press release by KCB Corporate Affairs on Friday, September 1, 2006.

Football Tournament Seeks to Bring Peace to Troubled Area

A football tournament set to start of the 30th August in Marsabit is being used as a means to bring different people groups together through the medium of sport. The tournament is being hosted in a region of Kenya that has seen drought and violence cause considerable instability and suffering to many communities. However, many hope that the Peace Cup will be a significant step in the road to reconciliation in an area that is currently fraught with division.

The tournament is the brainchild of a British student, James Griffin, who lived in the region for two and a half months last year working as a Christian missionary. Griffin found himself personally involved with the troubles after a horrific massacre in the village of Turbi, a village in which he himself had spent a considerable amount of time, claimed 76 lives last July. Griffin remembers that "it was heart-destroying to hear that so many people that I had met just weeks before had been so savagely killed", and so the establishment of the Peace Cup was an effort to contribute to the ongoing endeavors to make sure that such an event should never happen again.

Griffin has brought a team of other Christian students from the UK to play in the tournament and have been touring local schools in the area to encourage schools to give more time to sport in the area. The team has also been distributing over 300 footballs to schools and clubs so that teachers will be able to have the resources to include sports as part of the curriculum. "We are certain that the power of the gospel and football in young people's lives could bring about lasting peace in the area", says Griffin.

Teams will descend on Marsabit next Wednesday from all over Northern Kenya, with teams coming from the town itself, Moyale, Korr, North Horr, South Horr, Loyangalani and Logo, as well as Griffin's team from the United Kingdom.

The tournament has been generously supported by Kenya commercial Bank (KCB), the Anglican Church of Kenya (ACK), and the Kenyan Football Federation (KFF – Marsabit sub-Branch).

*****

SAFARI NJEMA: "GOOD SAFARI!"

September 8, 2006
Marsabit, Kenya
Final email from UK Football Team to friends and supporters

Our time in Kenya was really capped off by the successful end to the football tournament. Around 5,000 people came to the final, which apparently amounts to about 40% of Marsabit showing the community was supporting our endeavors. With our team – "Zion's Lions" – crashing out in the group stages thanks to a 5-0 drubbing at the hands of the eventual winners (who won the final 4-0, so we weren't THAT bad!), the team had some time to recuperate and spend some quality time at the touchline chatting with some of the spectators.

Our mission ended with a trip to a safari lodge in Samburu National Park which was wonderful – not least because we weren't fed rice and cabbage and we actually got proper toilets! It was fantastic to be able to relax together and enjoy seeing God's awesome creation – we saw elephants, a cheetah, lions, giraffes and many other animals in just two game drives so we were very blessed indeed.

Do please continue to pray for Northern Kenya – for the ongoing moves towards lasting peace between the ethnic groups and the efforts of the Anglican Church of Kenya, and other churches to share Christ with everyone, even in what can be tough conditions. It is an amazing part of the world, and none of us will forget our time there, and our support through prayer for the various ministries could really make a difference in many people's lives.

*****

SHORT-TERM MINISTRY: PRICELESS!

People return home from a short-term trip different. There is no other alternative. A person's perspective of the world is changed and that person will never be the same again. Mission teams energize the church and bring revival to both the host and sending churches. They instill a healthy sense of pride in the church and the lasting friendships team members build will last for a lifetime. Every single penny spent on short-term missions will come back ten-fold for God's Kingdom.

Following are short-term missionary letters from those who decided to leave their comfort zone and see what life is like in other parts of the world. This British group had a great system. Each person took one day writing for the team journal. When they got back to the UK they photocopied the journal and sent everybody copies. These excerpts from the Northern Kenya portion of their trip give us an additional perspective and angle from adult men and women of a variety of ages just days after James' group left.

September 17th 2006
Northern Kenya
David writes:

"The journey to Wadera was an experience by itself. We drove out of Marsabit past government offices, the prison and the hospital and out the bumpy and dusty road that was our route. We learned that prisoners' families are responsible for providing food for their relatives in jail! As we drove, we first encountered groups of women walking toward us carrying bags of charcoal, going into town to sell their produce. Our next meeting was heralded by a cloud of dust that covered the road ahead. It is remarkable how much dust a herd of cows can create. They were enroute to water.

The road became muddier and round thatched huts began to appear. These were Gabbra communities. This ethnic group has skins and plastic covering their huts instead of the 'mud and wattle' thatched buildings we had seen so far. With the fighting that has taken place between tribes these were refugees – displaced Gabbra people driven from their previous village setting up a new home.

The road continued its challenging course until we were in the middle of a crop, planted in rows on an open field. This was long-term cultivation of Miraa – the beloved narcotic of the Somalia and Arabs, providing income for the villagers of Wadera.

The village street was interesting as both sides of the road were lined with stockades containing dwellings, place for animals, raised storage areas (to keep out rats) and, of course, cooking areas. Having arrived early we were privileged to visit one home with brightly colored armchairs, plastic lino sheets on the floor and a decorated sack concealing the tin roof as a cloth ceiling. It was spotlessly clean.

The service, spoken in Boran, was led by the Rev. Elema with Rev. Todd robed and diligently at her side. It included songs sung from the young people and Sunday school and we performed a reduced version of our piece. After the service and much handshaking we mounted the Land Rover and set off with a grip of the handrails as tight as before!

On our return trip we saw many more animals on the road being herded in different directions. We failed to see neither the dead cows that had been spotted earlier nor the field of baboons that had been feeding beside the elephant fence at one point. We did, however, see the returning ladies and one was carrying a 5 foot length of fencing – presumably purchased from the proceeds of the charcoal."

*****

REVALE

Biddy writes: "When the day starts depends on which community you belong to in Marsabit. If you are Muslim, the muezzin beckons you to prayer at about 5 a.m. Perhaps this is why the two local Pentecostal groups have their praise sessions at a similar time. It is impossible not to hear them praising the Lord with great enthusiasm. The coming church bell wakeup call seems strangely ordinary! Todd leads a time of prayer and personal devotions in St. Peter's at 6:30 a.m. – a quiet start to the day if you can exclude the pigeons and crows dancing on the metal roof making a noise that sounds like stoning.

At about 10:15 we collected our packed lunch and water and piled into two Land Rovers. Todd had briefed us about the day last night and we learnt that most of the journey would be on the "newly graded" main road. We might have thought we were in for a smooth journey, but that would have been a false hope…on the great Cape Town to Cairo highway. No motorway boredom here!

*****

MEDICAL POINT OF VIEW

It is good to have a fact-finder take a turn writing the journal. Here are some excerpts from Mike's account of their trip to Bubisa.

Bubisa has "the 2nd deepest Sub Sahara well – approx 240 m. The population in the region is approx. 3,000. HIV in Kenya is a major issue and no less so here in the most northern part. Unfortunately the communities here are in denial and remark that HIV is a problem for Marsabit and not themselves. Apparently, the young men are encouraged to have intercourse with older married women outside the community in order to gain sexual experience before marriage. It is also common for married men to have a 'lady friend' outside the community too. In fact, it is considered 'a shame' if a married man has no other ladies apart from his wife. Thus, HIV Aids spreads rapidly. The promotion of faithfulness remains therefore a priority.

Female circumcision occurs between the ages of 12 to 15 and is not linked to marriage.

Male circumcision occurs between 17 and 18 years depending upon the next 'cycle' of circumcision. Generally this takes place at the health centre with one knife used per male rather than the previous practice of using a communal knife.

Health checks on infants are good, granting that the mother takes her child to the clinic.

Babies are weighed monthly up to 5 years, and every 6 months after that. Height and weight are also checked and monitored. Poor vision does not seem to be a major problem. Malaria protection is provided by nets being distributed. Infant mortality seems to be low. Throat cancer, high! Perhaps due to smoking and cooking from wood inside their huts.

*****

SORRY TO GO

"Time to go!!! I fell in love with the place. I felt at home and had such a sense of peace – not sure what this might mean!!! But the sadness of climbing aboard the Land Rover was soon replaced with the magnificent sight of camels – loads of 'em. Awesome!"

Tell me – I'll forget
Show me – I may remember
Involve me – I'll understand

- Mike

*****

STARK CONTRAST

"We said our farewells to Todd and Patsy and headed into Nairobi. Everything was a stark contrast to Marsabit – the vehicles, not-so-bumpy roads, the fumes, the people, and the buildings. It was hard to believe we were in the same country! Our room, toilet and shower felt like pure luxury after our recent experiences. In my room, there were several contented sighs! The evening drew to a close, and one felt very emotional. I was sad to be leaving Kenya, the people that I'd met and the friends I'd made." - Lucy

*****

The members of these short-term missionary groups from the USA and UK chose to leave their daily routine to embark on a journey to Africa. They took up their responsibility in global mission – living the Great Commandment of loving one another through the Great Commission of making disciples of all nations.

LESSONS LEARNED ALONG THE DETOUR:

Partnership is defined in the Greek word *enosis,* meaning "to unite, to link." The Book of Philippians is a biblical model of partnership between Paul and the Philippi church and their mutual partnership in ministry. "Their partnership involved mutual communication, financial support (Philippians 4:15), sending of laborers to work with Paul (Philippians 2:25), mutual prayer for each other (Philippians 1:4), mutual encouragement, expression of love, and special care during crisis/suffering times (Philippians 3:10).[xxx] "The body is a unit, though it is made up of many parts; and though all its parts are many, they form one body...now you are the body of Christ, and each one of you is a part of it" (1 Corinthians 12:12, 27). Through mission partnership we can experience cross-cultural oneness in Christ on a global scale.

DETOUR PRAYER:

Lord, help us to take up our responsibility in global mission. Living the Great Commandment, may we love and serve one another. While actively participating in the Great Commission, may we be committed to make disciples of all nations. Teach us to pray for missionaries and their partnering hosting and sending churches. Remind us to communicate with each other, maintaining significant contact, knowing prayer requests, encouraging them in their ministry doing what we can to assist. Help us to be willing to go when you call us and to the place where you call. And when we have experienced a short-term mission ourselves, help us to lead another group in order to give them the transformational encounter that we had the opportunity in which to partake. In Jesus' Name. Amen

CHAPTER NINE

ANOTHER BIG TURN IN THE ROAD!

Some minds are like concrete, thoroughly mixed up and
permanently set.

*****

July 7th 2006

In my life of transition...Marsabit...SJC...Marsabit...
SJC...what will be my stability and my anchor to keep the
boat from going adrift? My quiet times with the Lord.

Bishop Remi, from Madagascar, has written and asked us
to come back to Madagascar. Todd is on a list for election of
Bishop. I can't imagine leaving what we've started here. Yes,
what an honor. It is a new diocese that would reach the poorest
of the poor and we could make a difference to the country
in Madagascar, but to leave what we have here would be like

leaving Northern Kenya orphaned again! The people would be devastated, especially coming so soon after the death of Bishop Waqo!

Many times our love for those we minister to comes as a process. I've finally begun to gain compassion for the people in Northern Kenya. (Notice it doesn't always happen right away!) Yesterday, while at Karare, tears streamed down my face as I held babies on my lap and sang praise songs with the Samburu women and prayed over one whose chest was hurting. I believe she was healed – she got up and sang praise songs while we were there.

*****

BACK INTO THE DESERT?

The process of finding God's will in our move was a bumpy road, especially when our ministry was thriving in Northern Kenya. I did not understand. Why would God want to move us from something that was going so well? I felt like the Israelites would have – going from Egypt, where life was the land of plenty, back into the desert. Then I remembered it was also Egypt where they were in slavery! If I stayed in Kenya on my own terms then it would become like being enslaved to my own will instead of God's. I grappled over this thought for a period of time. Was I ready to go back into the desert?

*****

A CONVERSATION WITH THE LORD

The news that we might be leaving Kenya rocked my spiritual boat. Subconsciously I wanted to run away from the Lord, like a little girl hiding in her closet when hearing bad news from her parents. Finally, with the Lord's mercy and grace, He gently urged us to come out of our place of fear and trust in Him. There is no condemnation for those who are in Christ Jesus. Sometimes my journal entries were absent. I substituted prose, poems and free verse instead.

Here I am Lord.

I am pleased.

It's taken me so long to get back to you.

I am glad you've come.

I'm sorry. I've been so busy.

I am glad you have taken the time now.

I'm tired.

Come to me with your weary soul. I will give you rest.

It seems I try to make this a routine, but something always comes up.

It's not routine I am looking for. I'm looking for consistency…and a heart that worships God in spirit and truth.

I have come, Lord. Sometimes like as stubborn mule, stuck in mud, but here I am. Thank you for understanding me.

Why of course, my child! I am the one who created you…the one who formed you while you were in your mother's womb! I've created you with drive…with desire to achieve…with a will to succeed. Do not be ashamed!

But sometimes this "drive" slips into "overdrive" and pulls me away from you.

O my child….we could never be apart. Even when we are pulled, we are still together. I have made you to desire me and that's what will always pull us back together again. You are mine. You will always be mine. I love you with an everlasting love. I am glad I have created you. I look at my creation and am pleased. You are fearfully and wonderfully made.

*****

KEEP ME COMING BACK

Keep me coming back, Lord
Coming to you…
Running to you…
Sitting at the throne of grace…
Taking a rest from running the race…
Pausing a moment, setting the pace…
To come before You, face to face.
Keep me coming back, Lord.
Back to You.

*****

PASSION IS A PROCESS

Todd's new election as Missionary Bishop to Madagascar would cause our family of four to be in three separate countries. Todd in Madagascar, Charese in Kenya and Corbi would begin university study in the USA. Where did that leave me? Traveling from country to country; being like glue to hold our family together.

For several weeks I had not written in my journal (on purpose) because I'd not wanted to admit the pain and sorrow that would affect me if we left Kenya. Todd had a possible position of becoming bishop in Toliara, Madagascar. Although I would be happy for Todd – and I truly believed Todd is called to be Bishop someday – I would be sad to leave St. Julian's Centre and Kenya. My passion was to be in Kenya. I had a true love for SJC. Through a process and over a period of time I had also begun to receive a passion for the unreached people groups in Northern Kenya. *Lord*, I prayed, *cause my heart and mind to increase in love.*

Painstakingly, I began to journal, more as a discipline than a joy.

July 30ᵗʰ 2006 included the following:

"I am sure that if it was God's will for us to leave then I would gain my passion again for Madagascar. Of course I know that wherever the Lord takes us, my passion will grow, because like Paul, I will learn to be content in all things. Sometimes these passions are a growing process and don't come right away. But in some circumstances and events it is much quicker to learn! I have stated my passion before: to see SJC become its full potential in Christ, to spiritualize it, to offer retreats, workshops, teaching, times of worship and lead an edifying Sunday morning church service. I want this beautiful centre to be the spiritual hub for the ACK and beyond!

Yes, my sights are set on great things…great things because they are of God.

"In his heart a man plans his course, but the LORD determines his steps." I was reminded of Proverbs 16:9

My prayer became: Lord, not my will be done – but Thy will be done!

I know if the Lord took us back to Madagascar he would have an even greater plan because "For I know the plans I have for you," declares the LORD, "plans to prosper you and not to harm you, plans to give you hope and a future." Jeremiah 29:11. He wants the best for me and when I am willing to go to the point of death for His Kingdom, He will use me to my full potential.

I tried to be positive in my approach and optimistic in thoughts of returning to Madagascar. Even still, the times of darkness remained.

*****

IT'S DARK, LORD

Its dark, Lord
So dark I cannot even see your shadow.
I cannot see You face to face,
Even so, I know You are there
Guide me through the clouds
Like a GPS would guide a pilot.
I am flying an international plane
With many passengers
Kenya…USA…UK…Madagascar
I want not one person to get hurt
I have prayed for each one
And I hold them in my heart
Though the direction unclear,
Make Your way known
May Your will be done
On earth as it is in heaven.

*****

PRAYER: DON'T GIVE GOD INSTRUCTIONS - JUST REPORT FOR DUTY!

Many people want to serve God, but only as advisers. My conclusion on prayer, direction and discerning the will of God is this: When you have come to the end and know not even how to pray, pray this: "Thy will be done on earth as it is in heaven."

*****

OUR FATHER WHO ART IN HEAVEN

I cannot say "Our" if I live only for myself.

I cannot say "Father" if I do not endeavor each day to act like His child.

I cannot say "who art in heaven" if I am laying up no treasure there.

I cannot say "hallowed be thy name" if I'm not striving for holiness.

I cannot say "Thy kingdom come" if I'm not doing all in my power to hasten that wonderful event.

I cannot say "Thy will be done" if I am disobedient to His Word.

I cannot say "On earth as it is in heaven" if I'll not serve Him here and now.

I cannot say "give us this day our daily bread" if I'm dishonest or seeking things by subterfuge.

I cannot say "forgive us our debts" if I harbor a grudge against anyone.

I cannot say "lead us not into temptation" if I deliberately place myself in its path.

I cannot say "deliver us from evil" if I do not put on the whole armor of God.

I cannot say "Thine is the Kingdom" if I do not give the King the loyalty due Him from a faithful subject.

I cannot attribute to Him the power if I fear what men may do.

I cannot ascribe to Him the glory if I'm seeking honor only for myself and I cannot say "forever" if the horizon of my life is bound completely by time.

*****

GOD BELIEVES IN YOU!

August 13th 2006
St. Julian's Centre, Redhill, Kenya

Todd always reminds me: "We are told all our lives to believe in God…but I want to tell you something new. GOD BELIEVES IN YOU!"

I am glad for this. Right now, I am not sure I believe in myself and my ability to return to minister to the poorest of the poor. Like the story of the widow, all I have to offer are my two small coins. But what I do have, I give to the Lord. I pray He multiplies these coins and replaces them with His abundant riches from on high.

Todd also says: "I believe that God has revealed himself to every culture." I pray that He reveals Himself to me.

In all of this, I am searching for home.

WHAT IS HOME?

A place which is:

- familiar
- nurtured with love
- filled with peace and rest
- overflowing with friends
- a place of companionship
- bestowed with provisions for all our needs

(Notice it has nothing to do with a building.)

*****

NOT THE COLLAR, BUT THE CALL

August 25th 2006
St. Julian's Centre, Redhill, Kenya

We received an email yesterday from Bishop Remi. It was to Todd about his consecration, saying that he must speak with his wife about the issue of women's ordination, because the Province of the Indian Ocean doesn't (yet) ordain women. And here my ordination into the priesthood is just nine days away. I say I understand, but do I really?

We are not going to Madagascar for the purple, or the piety, but the passion for the people. Not the collar, but the call.

We are not going for fame or fortune but the unfortunate.

We are not going to push our own agenda but to be of service to others – to take the form of a servant.

Jesus is King but He didn't wear a crown. He took the form of a servant. I come as a priest, but I do not wear a collar. I take the form of a servant. You, Lord, have called me to serve.

I most probably will struggle with this more in Madagascar than I realize at this time while I am still wearing my collar in Kenya. Lord, give me grace, every step of the way.

*****

THE PRIESTHOOD OF BELIEVERS

Sunday, August 27th 2006
St. Julian's Centre, Redhill, Kenya

Last week Marietta Coleman (who is visiting Kenya with her husband, Robert) asked me how being ordained would change my life. A thought provoking question, especially when I explained that I really didn't think it would. In Madagascar they have not yet officially ordained women.

Having already been in ministry for 15 years on the mission field, I have received hands-on, practical training for servanthood. Although it was somewhat forced training at times, I have practical experience and I anticipate this will count for something! My hope and prayer is for this ordination to allow me to further my service for the Kingdom. As an ordained priest, I will be able to bless communion, baptize and marry. In the future, I hope to perform these sacraments in Madagascar, as true faith is set on what we do not yet see. Praise be to God!

I do realize it doesn't necessarily take a collar, or classes, to be set apart for His service. It takes a willing and obedient heart, wrapped in a blanket of love and compassion. All of God's children belong to the priesthood of the saints and are called to be set apart for His service. With or without the collar, we are all the priesthood of believers.

Jesus came in camouflage and revealed himself only to those who would believe. He had to purposefully give up his deity and replaced His crown with a cross to bear on our behalf. His sacrifice is still our example for today, in all cultures, in all conditions.

*****

SHATTERED

Journal Entry: Sept 21st 2006
St. Julian's Centre, Redhill, Kenya

The final reality. They have set the date. Todd's consecration to Bishop in Madagascar will be on Sunday, December 10th, 2006.

My heart cries out (and tears too!) "If only Todd would have liked it here at St. Julian's Centre! If only he would have caught the vision along with me – then we would have never had to move! Madagascar again?! Ugh! But I can't ask my husband to be any less than he is!"

I like Madagascar, but its hard living. And then, being in Tulear on top of that! So hot! Few friends – I don't even know ANYBODY!

My heart and flesh cry out to you! The uncompassionate side wants to whip me into shape. "Come on, Patsy. Get over it. Put your chin up. Get going and get a better attitude."

But my heart doesn't feel any better from that.

I want to be happy for my husband – it's such a great opportunity for him!

But what about all my visions, goals, desires, plans, dreams for St. Julian's Centre, Northern Kenya and a life here in Kenya?

Shattered - shot like a bullet in a window – only to have the pieces of glass shatter on the floor....like a piece of paper thrown into the shredder – lost – torn up – forever.

LESSONS LEARNED ALONG THE DETOUR:

What we think is permanent and secure in this world is only a transient piece of our earthly life and is never to be taken for granted. For me, I realized that I was coming off the detour, getting back on the main road of ministry in Madagascar. Whether I was willing or not willing, that was secondary. I had come to the realization that this was God's plan for me as His thoughts are not my thoughts and His ways are higher than our ways. (Is 55:8-9) First and foremost, he wants a broken and contrite heart as He is the potter and we are the clay. (Ps. 51:17)

DETOUR PRAYER:

Lord, as I struggle in understanding Your will for my life, help me to learn obedience, like Jesus did. (Heb 5:8) Help me to live a life worthy of the calling I have received. (Ephesians 4:1-3) In Jesus' Name I pray. Amen

CHAPTER TEN

MOVING ON

"The elephant does not get tired of carrying its tusks."
Massai Proverb

*****

This prayer was given to me by a friend in Kenya, although I did not understand the prayer at the time. A few months later, it seemed to be prophetic.

MOVING ON

Guardian, guide, no pillar of cloud by day nor fire by night,

Yet I sense Your presence with me, God of the journey

You are walking with me into a new land.

You are guarding me in my vulnerable moment.

You are dwelling within me as I depart from here.

189

You are promising to be my peace as I face the struggles of
distance from friends and Security, the planting of feet and
heart in a strange place.

Renew in me a deep trust in you. Calm my anxiousness.
As I reflect on my life I can clearly see
How you have been there in all of my leavings,
You have been here in all of my comings.
You will always be with me in everything.
I do not know how I am being resettled,
But I place my life into the welcoming arms of your love.

Encircle my heart with Your peace.
May your powerful presence run like a strong thread
Through the fibers of my being. Amen.

Author Unknown

*****

CHOSEN AND ORDAINED!

"You have not chose Me, but I have chosen you, and
ordained you, that ye would go and bring forth fruit, and that
your fruit should remain." John 15:16 KJV

Friends reminded me to reflect upon my ordination into
the priesthood, held on September 3rd, 2006. Every day at 4:07

p.m. I am reminded of the exact time the Archbishop Nzimbi and other ACK clergy laid hands on me as Todd's watch beeped for ten seconds during the middle of my ordination prayer!

Friends have inquired through email. "Do you feel any different?" "What had the most impact on you?" "Were your folks able to come?"

I praise God for the spiritual friendships that keep me on the path of accountability. We can too easily slip away if we are left alone on this journey of transforming into the image of Christ. I thank God for these "sacred companions." They are a gift.

Certainly it was a blessing by God that my parents and sister, along with two other friends were able to fly over from the States to celebrate with me on this special day. There were six Kenyans ordained into the priesthood and three ordained into the deaconate along with myself on that Sunday afternoon at All Saints Cathedral, Nairobi. The processional began at 1:00 p.m., African time. I think the long line of processionals (Mother's Union, cathedral choir, men's group, priests, ordinates, bishops, Archbishop) finally walked into the large stone church at 2:00 p.m. What a pleasure for me to see so many friends and supporters in the congregation!

Along with my family and friends from the USA were neighbors, congregants from the local church, St. Julian's Centre Management Committee Members, Heads of Staff and co-workers from the Anglican Church of Kenya, friends from RVA and Women at Ten (my women's Bible study), our

Doctoral Professor Dr. Robert Coleman and his wife, Marietta, and even missionary friends from Madagascar! Mom said my face just glowed. Seeing all those friends made me happy!

I think those who sat through the 3 ½ hour service deserve a prize, although the service didn't seem long to me. Throughout the entire service I sensed the peace of God. Even though I have been ordained into the priesthood, I am not a "churchy" person. I prefer to find God in a garden or on a golf course rather than with a lot of pomp and circumstance. But that day was something special. In a way, it was like getting married to the Lord – stating one's commitment to stay with Him for "better or for worse," "rich or poor,", "till death do us part" and for which neither height nor width nor death will be able to separate us from the love of God! In Him, there is no "death do us part!"

I have been meditating on a verse from Malachi 2:2, 6-7, "Set your heart to honor me. True instruction was in (her) mouth and nothing false was found on (her) lips. (She) walked with me in peace and uprightness and turned many from sin. For the lips of a priest are to preserve knowledge and from their mouth people should seek instruction because (she) is the messenger of the Lord Almighty."

Lord, help me to be a priest who has set my heart to honor You!

*****

EMAILS OF JUBILATION

Friends celebrated with us, sending emails of jubilation.

"This is to say blessings and prayers as you enter the ministry of priesthood. Your vocation was obvious given your leadership at St. Julian's. I hope these initial months have been full and rewarding.

And now back to Madagascar! I don't know what it means to have your bishop be your husband, but I'm sure you'll figure out how to support each other vocationally as you return to a place you know so well. What a ministry you have had at St. Julian's.

Well, my prayers are with you and your family as you say goodbyes and begin this next journey of faith and vocation.

Blessings and thanksgivings are with you at this time."

*****

This poem was on a card sent for my ordination from Christ Church, Charlevoix, Michigan. It seemed especially appropriate.

YOU ARE THE LORD'S

You are in God's place
At God's perfect time. Your
Days are in His hands, and he is

Your future. He has gifted you
And placed his hand upon you
To bless you and make you a
blessing. The burden of your
ministry is not yours to carry -
as you rest; he will work; as
you abide, He will bring fruit;
as you sow, He will give the
increase. He is your shield and
your exceeding great reward.

- Roy Lessin

*****

BEST CHEERLEADERS

Sept 16th 2006

Thank you for my parents, Lord Jesus. Thank You that they are physically strong enough to come to this barren land of Northern Kenya at the ages of 75 and 76. Thank You that their bodies are strong and limber and healthy to travel long distances and that they are willing to take all kinds of transportation – small planes, Land Rovers, trucks - able to balance and walk on uneven surfaces.

Thank you that they are committed to coming to visit, and for their loyalty and commitment to love one another and their family. Thank you for the growth in their spiritual lives and that they are hungering and thirsting for righteousness.

My parents did great while being here in Northern Kenya. "The personal value and unique gifts of a person needs affirmation. Ask questions and offer comments that will help individuals discover their potential."[xxxi] Thank you that through these years they have been two of my best cheerleaders.

*****

TODAY I AM DIFFERENT

Sept 23rd 2006
St. Julian's Centre, Redhill, Kenya

Today I am different; because of the prayers of the people. Last night we had a church meeting. Tiptons, Lays, Jeff and Mel, Roland and Jane Van Es, Todd and I. After eating our potluck supper and singing a few songs, we began our vision meeting for St. Julian's Chapel. The first thing I did was share my heart and the sadness in leaving St. Julian's Centre. I cried. They cried. Then they laid hands on me and we prayed.

"Spiritual friends nurture the development of each other's soul. Their love for each other translates into a desire that the other settle for nothing less than becoming all that he or she was intended to be. (They offer) the gift of themselves and their companionship on the transformational journey of Christian spirituality."[xxxii]

Today, even though the heart still hurts, I am different. Because of the prayers of my friends walking along with me on my spiritual journey, I notice a slight change for the better. It's almost indescribable. But it is there.

The Lord wants me to be real. He doesn't want me to put on a "happy" mask when I am devastated inside. He just wants me to be honest. Real.

There is a great cloud of witnesses watching – and praying. Like a professional golfer coming up to the 18th green, the pressure is on. But that's OK, because the Lord just wants me to play my game. The result is up to Him. Just play my game.

The Lord wants to develop character. Like the game of golf, that might mean practicing various aspects of our game.

"A character gap develops when we allow activity in the outer world to distract us from the daily business of bringing our attitudes, desires, words and behaviors under the sanctifying power of the Holy Spirit. Character is like physical exercise or any form of learning; you cannot "cram" hoping to do it in a day or week what can only be accomplished by months and years of consistent practice."[xxxiii]

I am amazed that the Paris Opera House, which sits on three acres of land, has four-fifths of its theater backstage… the backstage design ensures the onstage success. Just like the depth of our heart ensures outward obedience, we need to develop our hearts. Why does our heart throb? Lord, for me, let it be because of You.

*****

A GLOWWORM

"We are all worms. But I do believe I am a glow worm."
Winston Churchill

Monday, Sept. 24th 2006
St. Julian's Centre, Redhill, Kenya

Weaknesses. Nobody really wants to admit their weaknesses, but I think if we did, we would be more open and vulnerable. Life would be a lot less stressful. As Winston Churchill says, "We are all worms. But I do believe I am a glowworm."

Jesus calls us to a life of servanthood, not necessarily serving in our strength but only in our weaknesses. Actually, we are one beggar telling another beggar where to find bread - sinners serving sinners - people reaching people. There is not really anything special about us at all except through God who made us into His image. That is something special, not because of what we have done but rather because of who created us from the beginning.

The primary reason Jesus calls us to servanthood is not just because other people need our service. It is because of what happens to us when we serve. "Give yourselves to those who can bring you no status or clout. Just help people!"[xxxiv]

*****

NOT FIVE STEPS BEHIND

The transition was as tough as dried beef jerky. Asking friends to pray was imperative.

Sept 26th 2006
St. Julian's Centre, Redhill, Kenya
Email to friends and supporters

Hi to our dear friends. I am writing an email to you to ask you to pray for us. As you know, Todd and I are going through transition – he has been elected Bishop for Toliara. That means we are moving back to Madagascar! I realize that it will be a very big change for our family – and personally, I am not really excited about it, although I am happy for Todd. This is the desire of his heart, but I love it here at St. Julian's Centre and being around the girls. We could really use some prayers. As you know, transition rocks the boat for individuals and us as a couple. We are working through it – but could use some friends around to help us to pray and offer wise counsel. I do have girlfriends who are godly and guide me as I process this and pray.

A woman's and man's point of view are poles apart. Todd has a totally different opinion about our move to Madagascar. Individually as male and female, we are looking at our move from very different angles.

I am trying not to be selfish, but I do realize that I am a woman with normal feelings and concerns. One of them being long periods of separation and finding "home." Leaving friends in Kenya, and transitioning back to Madagascar where life is more difficult, less comfortable and severely taxing will take strength. I would be most grateful if you would keep us in your prayers.

I also wanted my parents to come to Africa and spend more time here. Thinking SJC to be the perfect place, we even considered buying property to build a house! Now our move to Madagascar has changed our plans! Since the medical facilities are next to nothing there, especially in Toliara, it won't be possible to have my aging parents stay there for several months at a time.

Personally I am wondering what I am going to do in Madagascar when my heart is here. God will reveal it in His time, but the process is not always easy to go through, especially for a woman, when many times the man is leading. I want to go hand in hand with my hubby – not five steps behind.

*****

A VOTE OF THANKS

My leadership team is praying with me about all the changes. The staff here at St. Julian's Centre is resilient and fun to work with. They have grown so much in their professional endeavors over the past three years. Most of the kinks have been worked out, although there will always be some. They do need an overseer, an encourager, someone who can market SJC and has vision as well as leadership skills to guide the staff. Finances will always have to be scrutinized.

Words of appreciation don't always come in one's place of work. Certainly we are thankful when they do. This letter was handwritten from the Sr. Staff of Security, Anthony, whose mother tongue is not English. It's a keeper.

Hi Mama this is Anthony.

I want to thank you for taking us out for three days (Mombasa) to enjoy ourselves together with you without separating one another. We do enjoy very much. Especially me myself to swim in the OCEAN! Just Imagine? Anthony in the OCEAN swimming! Fantastic! That marks something in my heart which I will never forget and thank you to Mama to take the responsibility to show me how to swim.

Thank you again mama to fulfill your promise coz people don't believe that day will came and get themselves (to) Mombasa.

But the dream came true thing. Mama for this period you are here I hope you will make everybody to know this country well.

I have much more to thank you about. The Mombasa retreat but let me stop there. May God bless your family and live peaceful lives on this planet (earth).

Yours faithfully,
Anthony Wanjala Juma

"Let the blessing "Mama" all days on your life in this world."
11.03.2007

*****

I CHOOSE TO SERVE

One of the things I have personally been dealing with this time around is "choices." I didn't feel like I had a choice in all this. I felt like I was to just follow Christ, leave everything behind and blindly go! But the Lord is a compassionate God and He holds our hand through the process. One day while in my office at St. Julian's Centre, I wiped the dust off a CD and put it in my computer. The first song reminded me that we do have a choice! *"I Will Choose Christ!"* by Kathy Tricoli. Bingo! I do have a choice! The choice is – whether or not to choose Christ. Whether or not to be willing to go where He has chosen us to go! Even though I might not choose which country or environment I might be in…I still do have a choice — I will choose CHRIST!

A CHOICE
by Patsy McGregor

A choice I have to make today
To serve the flesh or go God's way
A new day dawning, a new choice to make
Who do I serve? What choice do I make?

I can choose to die or I can choose to live.
Choose to receive or choose to give.
Choose to sulk or choose to sing.
Choose to praise God for everything.

Choose to obey or go my own way.
Choose to encourage and watch what I say.
Choose to love God or serve my own flesh.
The decision I make - may our Lord bless.

So now in the morning, I pause and I pray
To listen to God and hear what He says.
To make my decision on what I will do
For my actions determine my life through and through.

LESSONS LEARNED ALONG THE DETOUR:

We do have a choice! Not necessarily a choice in circumstances, or environment, or financial stability but in our attitudes and who we follow. What will your choice be today? For me, I choose Christ!

DETOUR PRAYER:

Lord. Help me make the right choices. So far today, I have not yelled at anybody, not gotten angry nor mistreated a soul. I have treated everybody I have encountered today with love and respect. Now, I am going to get out of bed, and I will need more help. Dear Lord, reign in me! Teach me to choose Christ! In Jesus' Name, I pray. Amen.

CHAPTER ELEVEN

FULL SPEED AHEAD

We dance, therefore we are.

(African proverb)

*****

MAY I HAVE THIS DANCE?

Imagine you and the Lord Jesus are walking along the beach together.

For much of the way the Lord's footprints go steadily, consistently, rarely varying in the pace. But your prints are in a disorganized stream of zig zags, starts, stops, turnarounds, circles, departures, and returns. For much of the way it seems to go like this. But gradually, your footprints come in line with the Lord's, soon paralleling His consistently. You and Jesus are walking as true friends.

This seems perfect, but then an interesting thing happens: your footprints that once etched the sand next to the Master's are now walking precisely in His steps. Inside His large footprints is the smaller "sandprint," safely enclosed. You and Jesus are becoming one. This goes on for many miles.

But gradually you notice another change. The footprints inside the larger footprints seem to grow larger. Eventually it disappears altogether. There is only one set of footprints. They have become one. Again this goes on for a long time.

But then something awful happens. The second set of footprints is back. This time it seems even worse than before. Zig Zags all over the place. Stop...start. Deep gashes in the sand. A veritable mess of prints. You're amazed and shocked. But this is the end of your dream.

Now you speak: *"Lord, I understand the first scene with the zig zags, fits, starts, and so on. I was a new Christian, just learning. But You walked on through the storm and helped me learn to walk with You."*

"That is correct," replied the Lord.

"Then, when the smaller footprints were inside of Yours, I was actually learning to walk in Your steps. I followed You very closely."

"Very good. You have understood everything so far."

"Then the smaller footprints grew and eventually filled in with Yours. I suppose that I was actually growing so much that I was becoming more like You in every way."

"Precisely."

"But this is my question, Lord. Was there a regression of something? The footprints went back to two, and this time it was worse than the first."

The Lord smiles, then laughs. *"You didn't know?"* He says, *"That was when we danced."*[xxxv]

*****

I SEE PINK, HE SEES BLUE

Through our transition, I was reminded of the many differences between male and female. I summed it up six words. I see pink. He sees blue.

Dr. Emerson Eggerichs, author of *Love and Respect,* writes of the basic need for a woman to be loved by a man. For a man, he needs respect. He describes the man's desire and need to be head of the relationship and the importance that the woman appreciates her husband's desire to work and achieve.[xxxvi]

I see this in my relationship with Todd. I see through pink sunglasses and he sees through blue. Only a few weeks ago he returned from furlough in the USA – after being gone from Kenya almost six months. Our entire family had been in different places for the past several months and we had been separated from the end of August to the end of November. I, in my pink sunglasses, exclaimed, *"Praise God! We are finally together as a family!"*

For Todd, he sees blue. Not even a week after he returned, he called Mission Aviation Fellowship (MAF) to book a flight to Northern Kenya. In his blue sunglasses he has an inborn desire to work and achieve. This is the way God has created him. Through his blue sunglasses, he had not been in Northern Kenya for over six months! Imagine an "executive" being away from the office more than six months! As a wife, I needed to take off my pink sunglasses and see through his blue ones. I needed to respect his desire to work and achieve – and even more so to this humble man of God who does not seek fame or fortune but who is willing to work in dire circumstances wherever God places him in this world!

According to Eggerichs, a man has a "natural, inborn desire to go out and conquer the challenges of this world – to work and achieve. As a wife, if she can start to understand how important her husband's work is to him, she will take a giant step toward communicating respect and honor, two things her husband values more than love."[xxxvii]

Gen. 2:18 "The LORD God said, 'It is not good for the man to be alone. I will make a helper suitable for him.'" Hebrew for 'helper' means literally, "a help answering to him." 1 Cor. 11:9 "neither was man created for woman, but woman for man."

"From the very beginning, man was called upon to 'work in the field' and to provide for his family. The male feels a deep need to be involved in adventure and conquest. This is not an option for him; it is a deep seated trait."[xxxviii]

I guess the best option is not to put either pair of sunglasses away, but to keep both pairs available and close at hand. This combination would allow us to see the color purple. After all, isn't this the color a Bishop is to wear?

*****

TREASURE OF FRIENDSHIP

A trusting friend brings fullness of life,
the person who gets one has a treasure.
- Swahili Proverb

Thank God for treasures in friendship! "Christian spirituality demands journeying together. This means more than the accompaniment of the Spirit of God. It also includes the accompaniment of fellow pilgrims."[xxxix] Thank God for modern technology and email which makes this gift of spiritual friendship available even when we are oceans apart.

Encouragement is the oxygen of the soul."[xl] Thank You God for the prayers of people which breathes life into our inmost beings.

From Cindy: *"Patsy, I sensed your prayer request in my heart even before I saw your email (and have been praying already!) I sensed this was going to be the most difficult transition for you and Todd, especially pertaining to the girls and being near to them while in Kenya. Please know I'll be praying for your communication to be open, tempered with God's Spirit, for listening and caring ears, for God's Word to filter through truths, for the enemy to not have a stronghold in any way in this and for your heart to be open and heard. At school this week your family was lifted up during our "See you at the Pole" prayer time (an all-school, before school prayer event.) One of the moms afterwards was so struck by your story (she's a pastor's wife) and is praying for you already, too!"*

*****

From Graham and Sherry: *"Thank you so much for writing. You always have our prayers and love. We feel very close to you though the Lord has us so far apart geographically. Sherry and I have already talked and prayed about your concern. It occurred to us as well. I'm sure the Lord's peace will come but it may well take some time. I am planning to be there for the consecration on December 10ᵗʰ leaving earlier that week, but Sherry is unable to come. All our love."*

*****

From Barb: *"Hey, so good to hear from you. I am sure there has been some challenges in facing this "about face" in your life. Please write a book about it, because we all need to be ready for an "about face" situation in our lives as well."*

*****

THE MAYONNAISE JAR AND COFFEE

When things in your life seem almost too much to handle, remember the mayonnaise jar and coffee…

A professor stood before his philosophy class and had some items in front of him. When the class began, wordlessly, he picked up a very large and empty mayonnaise jar and proceeded to fill it with golf balls. He then asked the students if the jar was full. They agreed that it was.

So the professor then picked up a box of pebbles and poured them into the jar. He shook the jar lightly. The pebbles rolled into the open areas between the golf balls. He then asked the students again if the jar was full. They agreed it was.

The professor next picked up a box of sand and poured it into the jar. Of course, the sand filled up everything else. He asked once more if the jar was full. The students responded with a unanimous "*yes.*"

The professor then produced two cups of coffee from under the table and poured the entire contents into the jar, effectively filling the empty space between the sand. The students laughed.

"*Now,*" said the professor, as the laughter subsided, "*I want you to recognize that this jar represents your life. The golf balls are the important things – your God, family, your children, your health, your friends and your favorite passions – things that if everything else was lost and only they remained, your life would still be full.*

The pebbles are the other things that matter like your job, your house and your car.

The sand is everything else – the small stuff.

"*If you put the sand into the jar first,*" he continued, "*there is no room for the pebbles or the golf balls. The same goes for life. If you spend all your time and energy on the small stuff, you will never have room for the things that are important to you. Pay attention to the things that are critical to your happiness. Play with your children. Take time to get medical checkups. Take your partner out to dinner. Play another 18. There will always be time to clean the house and fix the disposal."*

"Take care of the golf balls first, the things that really matter. Set your priorities. The rest is just sand."

One of the students raised her hand and inquired what the coffee represented.

The professor smiled. *"I'm glad you asked. It just goes to show you that no matter how full your life may see, there's always room for a couple of cups of coffee with a friend."*

*****

ARE YOU FIT?

Now that I was choosing to move back to Madagascar, I needed to take some spiritual inventory. I wanted to glean from my years at St. Julian's and account for the array of life lessons and managerial skills I had developed. I wanted to catalog my strengths, weaknesses, passions, dislikes and take stock for the next several years of missionary service in Madagascar.

I realized that even though my husband and I had different gifts, we were both still gifted. I had an identity of my own. I had to start whittling the face of that piece of wood, my identity. What did it look like? I was encouraged by Eph. 4:11-12

"It was he who gave some to be apostles, some to be prophets, some to be evangelists, and some to be pastors and teachers, to prepare God's people for works of service, so that the body of Christ may be built up." What are my gifts? How can I use those gifts to build up the body of Christ? My life and ministry at St. Julian's Centre caused me to take inventory of my spiritual SHAPE.

On October 10th of every year there is the Grass Courts Championship in Limuru, Kenya at the home of Michael and Diana Shaw. This particular year was the 50th anniversary of this classic event and Todd and I had the opportunity to be two of the 24 people invited to play, including 12 men and 12 women. Partners are drawn out of a hat and placed into one of two pools. Each team plays 11 games against the other teams in their pool. Five teams' times 11 games equal 55 games. Then if one happens to make it into the finals (like I did ☺) that means another set against the winner of the other pool to determine the tournament champion.

My partner, whom I had never met before, and I began to walk on the court for our very first match. He turned his head, swinging his racquet and said, *"Are you fit?"* (You could tell he was a Brit.) Basically what he was saying is, "Are you ready for all this tennis? Are you in shape?" At the beginning of the match I might have said, "Sure, why not!" If you would have asked me a few days after I played 64 games of hard tennis in one day, my answer might have been different.

Are we spiritually fit? Are we ready for the long haul? Can we persevere through hard times? Do we know our gifts and talents so that we can serve the body of Christ to the glory of God? Lord, help us to be aware of our SHAPE in ministry.

*****

ARE YOU IN 'SHAPE?'

Rick Warren, the author of *The Purpose Driven Life* explains the acronym of SHAPE.

S – Spiritual gifts
H – Heart
A – Abilities
P – Personality
E – Experience

He says, "God has deliberately shaped and formed you to serve Him in a way that makes your ministry unique." Nobody can do it like you can! God uses all of our life to mold us for ministry to others and shape us for our service to Him. What SHAPE are you in?

We had a clock in Marsabit that would not keep time. Why it was still called a clock is something to be debated. First, I thought the clock did not work because it needed a battery, so I went to the *duka* and purchased two double AA's. I was relieved when I began hearing *tick tick*. But several hours later, I looked at the clock and noticed that although it was still ticking, the hands were not moving. It was not keeping time. The clock had motion, but no movement.

Have you ever noticed this in your personal life or life of ministry? Motion without movement – like life on a treadmill, running, but not going anywhere? When we are not aware of our SHAPE in ministry, we will experience frustration. We will have motion (doing things) but not making progress. Motion without movement. a spiritual road block on the journey of life.

*****

I AM AN ENTHUSIAST!

During a women's retreat at St. Julian's we studied the Enneagram Personality Test. We intentionally considered our gifts, strengths, weaknesses, personalities and other aspects of *self*. After several calculations in response to a multitude of questions, I learned that I am an enthusiast - one who wants to celebrate joy in life! I also read carefully Gary Thomas' *Sacred Pathways* which uses personality temperaments in discovering a person's pathway to God. And what have I learned?

Enthusiasts: Loving God with Mystery and Celebration

The blessings of an enthusiast are: 1) dreams – and within that is the importance of journaling, community, meaning and perspective 2) expectancy and 3) prayer.

The book explains that the enthusiast is fed through celebration! They enjoy enthusiastic worship. They are energized by children because children help us recapture the joy and wonder of our faith. The enthusiast enjoys creating! Whatever it is – scrapbooking, writing a song, cooking a meal, rearranging the house, playing guitar - CREATE. Enthusiasts must take care to remain solid in Bible teachings and Scripture reading. Mystery and celebration are good, but we must also remain rooted in good, Biblical training. The enthusiast needs both feeling and reason to get full meaning out of Scripture reading.

We are warned not to seek experience for experience's sake and it also cautions us not to become too independent. Enthusiasts "perhaps more than any other temperament, need to be rooted in a strong church that can hold individual believers accountable."[xli]

"Feelings come and go. Enthusiasts shouldn't apologize for enjoying them, but they should avoid being dependent upon them."

Have you identified your spiritual gifts and passions? Are you in SHAPE? Let us all find our own identity in Christ and use the gifts that He has given us for His service and for His honor and glory.

*****

WE HAVE TO DO WHAT WE HAVE TO DO!

Someone once told me that I was a "remarkable woman."

- a road builder
- policewoman
- security guard
- detective
- author
- administrator
- priest
- prayer warrior

I just say "We have to do what we have to do!"
(Including teaching people how to swim!)

*****

A MASSAI WARRIOR LEARNS HOW TO SWIM

It's not only the westerners who are encouraged to get out of their comfort zone and try something new. The staff of St. Julian's Centre took a retreat to Mombassa and I urged several of them to come with me – into the Indian Ocean.

The challenge in teaching someone to swim, especially float, is a matter of trust. (I learned this in college as a Health and Physical Education major.) To teach them to lie on their backs, put their head - especially ears - in the water, and spread out their arms like Jesus did on the cross requires courage. From this position they take a deep breath and slowly, as their bodies stay afloat, I remove my hand from underneath the small of their back. As they gain confidence they can then do it themselves. All it requires is trust.

For Kopito, the challenge was even greater. I not only had to gain his trust to teach him how to float, but also to get him in the water. This strong Massai warrior, who had killed a lion with only a spear, felt the first wave, almost fell and grabbed my hand as I led him to the knee-deep ocean. Like a body stiffened with rigor mortis, he would hardly bend. Fear finally was overcome by trust and he began to float. What a joy for him to finally learn what it was like to rest on top of water!

Lord, help us to rely on You to overcome our fears in life and give us heartfelt joy when we finally learn to rest in Your loving arms.

*****

PRAYING GOLF

I would never say that the game of golf is easy. However, it is *easier* to play the same course over and over. Then we know what to expect, we know yardages, clubs to hit, and are more apt to read the green, determining direction the putt will break. The challenge comes when we play a different course.

The par three at Mt. Kenya Safari Club was shorter, but not easier for me. There were new distances, new "greens", and new breaks. The first time playing this diminutive course was quite intimidating. I didn't know anything! But playing the course a second time around allowed me to learn from my mistakes. I still miss-hit shots, but at least I knew the direction of the flag and which club would take me there.

My thoughts began to ponder, and my score began to soar! Maybe that's what Madagascar would be like the second time around. On the tiny par 3, we would have to hit over brush – blinding us at the tee from sight of the hole. I depended upon my caddie for every shot on the course. He gave the distance, I chose my club. I might even forget my previous club and he would pull it out of bag, smile, and hand it to me.

This is the game of life. Sometimes we get too comfortable and play the same game on the same course in our own strength. Then God might bring us a challenge, a new course, to cause us to grow in our game, to work on new area. On the par 3 it was my short game that needed work. Forget about the putting, there was no rhyme or rhythm to the greens!

With this in mind, Toliara, Madagascar, will be a totally new course of life. It has its own challenges to bring new growth and those who know me will agree - I am a woman who thrives on challenges and competition! I like the race of life! I will sharpen my skills and grow in the process. The Lord will be my caddie to guide me along this new course of life.

*****

VISUALIZE YOUR TARGET

Since my thoughts were on a roll, the next morning I arose early, walked to the Mt. Kenya Safari Club golf course and *prayed* another nine for my personal time with the Lord. I don't remember my score, but I gleaned the following analogies of how golf was similar to life.

- Golf, like life, is a game of details
- Take notes: if there is no time for note-taking, you are playing too fast
- Learn from mistakes
- Don't take it too seriously - we are "only practicing" – advised my one armed caddie from Limuru, George
- Enjoy the journey, work through the detour
- Don't expect too much first time around
- Life, like a golf course, can be very intimidating
- Don't give up
- Find your strength and focus on the positive
- Improve your weakness
- Duplicate the good

- Learn from what didn't work (Edison said he never failed at inventing the light bulb – it was just a 2,000 step process!)
- Practice correctly, perfect practice makes perfect
- Not every shot is going to be perfect
- Give new things a try (the caddie gave me a 7 iron on the edge of the green!)
- New equipment is not always the key
- Don't judge the next shot from the tee box
- Remove the obstacles in line with your goal (branch, leaf, clump of dirt)
- KIP – Keep it Positive
- VISUALIZE YOUR TARGET – "The spot where you want your ball to finish is the target, and by being aware of that spot, you give your swing direction."
- Lord, help me visualize my target in the game of life.

*****

<<<<<<<<<<<<<<<<<<<<<<<<<<<<<<<<<<<<<<<<<<<<<<<<

I was beginning to accept our move to Madagascar. It seems like Todd's missionary call began before he was born. As described in Psalm 139:13, 16, "You created my inmost being. You knit me together in my mother's womb…You saw my unformed body. All the days ordained for me were written in your book before one of them came to be."

BEFORE YOU WERE BORN
By Todd Andrew McGregor

As I look back, there are a number of experiences where God was preparing me for my new ministry as Bishop of Toliara in Madagascar. But if I were to choose two experiences which seem to impress me above the other, they would be an Episcopal Renewal Conference in Kanuga, NC and a class at Seabury Western Theological Seminary where we took the Myers-Briggs Personality Test.

It was in the mid 1990's when a woman spoke words of knowledge to me during a Renewal Conference at Kanuga Conference centre in North Carolina. I, along with four others, were chosen out of 400 to come forward in front of the congregation as the rest of the participants began to use their gifts of discernment, words of knowledge, and prophecy regarding the five of us.

The wife of the guest speaker, Bishop David Pytches, spoke the following words of knowledge, even though we had never met. "I don't know what this means, but I see the word 'Apostle' flashing before my eyes. Apostle, Apostle, Apostle."

My thought at that time was that it referred to the Greek meaning, "one who is sent out." It reminded me of my missionary call. But as I was sharing this with other Episcopal friends, one clergy said, "Apostle in the Anglican tradition refers to the Bishop, as the chief clergy."

About a year later, I was attending Seabury Western Theological college for an Anglican studies Program. Our class took and discussed the Myers-Briggs Personality Test. Out of approximately 25 students, I was the only person who had a certain combination of traits. The professor stated, "This type of person usually becomes Bishop in the Episcopal church." So, my classmates made a small paper mitre and placed it on my head.

These two events left an indelible impression on me and foreshadowed my consecration. On December 10, 2006, at 9:30 a.m. St. Laurent Cathedral in Antananarivo was overflowing with over 1,000 people and another 200-300 standing outside the cathedral walls. Leading the celebration was Archbishop of the Indian Ocean, The Most Rev. Ian Ernest, six other bishops from the Province of the Indian Ocean (including our leader for 12 years, the Rt. Rev. Remi Rabenirina), along with Bishop Leo Frade from the diocese of Southeast Florida. Joining the Bishops were over 80 clergy and evangelists from the Diocese of Antananarivo.

Also present was the Prime Minister of Madagascar, the President of the National Assembly, the American and Mauritian Ambassadors, representatives from the Catholic, Reform, and Lutheran churches, missionary friends, my brother Tom, my mentor the Rev. Graham Smith, good friends the Rev. Colin Preece from the Diocese of Canterbury and Scott Purdy from Chicago, my wife, children and in-laws Gerry and Audrey Cox, Kenya friends Donna and Ethan Coots and loads of Malagasy friends.

The service was breathtaking as we combined both Malagasy and English for the service. Patsy blessed us with a song she wrote, entitled, "Follow Me." The President of the National Assembly liked the song so much that he requested another song from Patsy at my installation service in Toliara on January 17th, 2007.

One of the questions I thought about during my consecration was how many Bishops does it take to dress a new bishop? For me, it was eight! Each one of them gave me another part of my "uniform". One gave me my ring, another the cross, another a cope, another the mitre, another the staff, another the stole, another the Bible and the Archbishop gave me the charge. This is a true reminder that we all have a part to play in the body of Christ and the networking of His Church!

Bishop Frade from the Diocese of Southeast Florida gave a superb sermon regarding the 12 spies going into Canaan, the Promised Land (Numbers 13-14). The spies saw that the Promised Land was fruitful and flowing with milk and honey.

However, most of the spies were pessimists, saying the Canaanites were too strong." We can't attack those people they are stronger than we are...we seemed like grasshoppers I our own eyes and we looked like the same to them." But Caleb and Joshua, faithful and godly men, silenced the other spies, elders and community by saying, "We should go up and take possession of the land, for we can certainly do it...if the Lord is pleased with us, he will lead us into that land, a land flowing with milk and honey and will give it to us...and do not be afraid of the people of the land."

This is a great reminder that even though we may look like grasshoppers in the eyes of people, we are more than conquerors in the eyes of the Lord when we live a life worthy of God's calling. Just as the Lord has guided in the past, He will also lead us in the future as we rise up and take possession of that which the Lord has already given us!

An Apostle is to be sent forth to new frontiers with the gospel, providing leadership over church bodies and maintaining authority over spiritual matters pertaining to the church.

*****

MASTER'S PIECE

"Humility is the decision to 'let God be God.'"
- Martin Luther

Finally, peace amidst the storm. On Thursday, March 15, 2007, when Todd was already in Madagascar, I wrote this email to my hubby.

Hi Hon,

How was your trip to Sakaraha? I am sure the Lord was working in marvelous ways. He is an awesome God.

Corbi, Charese and I fasted on Tuesday because they left today on the bus to go to interim safari (week long class field trip) and did not want to fast Wednesday on the bus. (During the Lenten season, our family has a disciplinary custom to fast one day a week together.) I had an amazing day with the Lord on Tuesday. The Spirit of the Lord was so strong upon me that I could hardly move. I was here at SJC, and went out to the big field with two mats. I laid prostrate before the Lord for about half an hour. Then I walked to my office and then to the chapel. The Spirit was so strong upon me that I could hardly walk. All I could do was sit before Him. I went to the chapel to sing, and could hardly sing. I went out to the grounds to walk and could hardly walk. All I could do was sit before His throne.

I felt like I was paralyzed in His presence and the love of God. I felt revival was coming, just like I have been reading about in both Charles Finney's and Robert Coleman's books.

In the chapel I sensed, once again – this also happened to me last Saturday - that I need to be ready to go to Madagascar sooner than expected. We are awaiting Charese's graduation in July 2008, but what is keeping me from coming before that? Financial strains? Educational concerns? Medical coverage?

Concerns about Charese being in Kenya alone? Housing in Mada?

Yes, I would say to all the above, but actually when it boils down to it, these are concerns and worries of the world. The Lord has been speaking Matt. 6:26 to me. Consider the birds of the air, they do not toil, nor spin nor store up in barns, but I take care of them. Are you not more important than they? Charles Finney talks about "fallow ground" in his book *Lessons On Revival* – ground which was toiled before but, for one reason or another, has hardened. I was contemplating this and wondering what the "fallow ground" is in my life, especially in leading and living the Great Commission. John Wesley's words also came to me, "Don't only go to those who need you. Go to those who need you most." This reminded me of our loved ones in Madagascar who need us most.

The bottom line is that I now WANT to join you in Madagascar and as soon as possible – which could probably be November 2007. I cannot give you an earthly reason why I want to go, besides being with you. The reason must be that God is changing my heart. He is the potter, I am the clay. Make me and mold me. This is what I pray. Change my heart, O God.

From a "worldly view" this doesn't make sense, but we do not look as the world does, but as God does. As I look out my office window, I could not have a lovelier place. Beautiful grounds, lovely environment, peaceful, quiet and friendly. St. Julian's is a beautiful place, a masterpiece in my eyes. It has so much potential. I have brought it to the Promised Land but it is another person's responsibility to cross over and take it further. That is not my river to cross and I am willing to let it go.

I wasn't at this point on Saturday. I drove up to RVA for volleyball practice and was early so walked around the field overlooking the Great Rift Valley and Mt. Longonaut. Again, I could hardly walk and felt "paralyzed in His presence." I lay on the grass and prayed. I sensed the Lord telling me to let St. Julian's go. I didn't want to. I imagined myself a great artist (that is an imagination!) who had a vision, the ability, the desire and the passion to paint a beautiful painting, a masterpiece, which someday, could be placed in a museum for all to see. As the artist, I had begun that painting and was pleased with my work, because I knew that it was really the Lord working through me for His glory – creating, painting and giving me the talents to cause this to be a beautiful masterpiece.

But the time came for me to give the painting away. It wasn't finished! I was like the university student who knew all the answers but ran out of time to complete the test! How frustrating! On top of the disappointment, I was unsure what was going to happen to the beautiful masterpiece which I had spent the past several years developing. It was a half-painted canvas with the lines drawn in but it was no longer my responsibility to finish. I must now trust the Creator to bring somebody else to finish what had been started and it is hard to let go. What if they leave the painting in a closet to mildew, gather dust and never complete? Or set it outside for the elements to weather and ruin? Or the worst-case scenario – given away just for someone to bring an old crayon to scribble away and ruin the work already begun!

Then I realized the painting was never mine to keep. At the beginning, I knew it was for a greater purpose, for others to enjoy. But I liked the painting so much myself I wanted to dwell in it, keep it in my own house so that I could enjoy its beauty all the days of my life! But once again, the painting was never mine to own and I must be willing to give it away, as it was meant to be given in the first place.

I guess the Lord is gently opening my tight fist one finger at a time, to give this painting to the ones to whom it belongs. I am now at the point that I have an open hand, extending it unto the Lord, and I know it is time to move on. I will join you in Madagascar as soon as the Lord takes this masterpiece out of my extended, open hand, for it has become my offering back to Him. After all, He is the Master and each one of us is just His piece, making us all a Master's piece.

I love you. Your Queen of Hearts.

LESSONS LEARNED ALONG THE DETOUR:

Our life is too short to rebel, to argue, to want our own way. The detour to Kenya was God's preparation time and a blessing to us. During these five years I discerned my spiritual gifts. It allowed Todd to return to his true calling of grass roots ministry and serving the poorest of the poor. It allowed new scenery, a good education for Corbi and Charese and good family times while the girls were at boarding school. We were able to make new contacts, meet new friends and network with the body of Christ. We found our passion in hosting short-term mission groups and providing an opportunity for people to gain practical mission experience. It was a valuable, bumpy ride.

DETOUR PRAYER:

Revive us, O Lord! As we humble ourselves, pray, seek your face and turn from our wicked ways. May You hear our prayer, forgive our sins and heal our land. (2 Chronicles 7:14) In Jesus' Name, I pray. Amen.

CHAPTER TWELVE

DETOUR COMPLETE

"He who deliberates fully before taking a step
will spend his entire life on one leg."
Chinese Proverb

*****

January 2nd 2008
Ankilifaly, Toliara, Madagascar

When looking through human eyes at the life of Joseph in the book of Genesis, we see setback after setback.

"From God's point of view, he was being carefully prepared for his life's calling and destiny. We are often concerned about getting a task finished. God is concerned about getting the person prepared so that he or she can finish the task. We want a job done; God wants a person molded. We want to work for God; God desires to work on us."[xlii]

As I lie on my bed with the fan in my face in 100 degree weather, I ponder these thoughts and stare out my window to the slum next door. God's not going to change these circumstances for quite a while. Purchasing land, obtaining the titles, and building a house and cathedral will take years. So, in order to be comfortable, I am going to have to change. My circumstances won't, but I will have to.

I was moved this morning in my quiet time as I read Heb. 11:8, "By faith Abraham, when called to go to a place he would later receive as his inheritance, obeyed and went, even though he did not know where he was going." Oswald Chambers comments,

"There is no logical answer possible when anyone asks you what you are doing. One of the most difficult questions to answer in Christian work is "What do you expect to do?" You don't know what you are going to do. The only thing you know is that God knows what He is doing. Continually examine your attitude toward God to see if you are willing to "go out" in every area of your life, trusting in God entirely. It is this attitude that keeps you in constant wonder, because you don't know what God is going to do next."[xliii]

"Security depends not so much on how much you have, as upon how much you can do without."[xliv]

The German pastor Dietrich Bonhoeffer wrote from prison during the Nazi regime of Adolf Hitler, "I'm sure everything that happens to me has a purpose, even if it cuts across our own wishes. As I see it, I am here for some purpose and I only hope I'm living up to it. In the light of our supreme purpose, all our personal privations and disappointments are trivial."[xlv]

Lord, help me remember this along my journey here in Ankilifaly, Toliara. My hope is in You. You are my All in All.

*****

EMBRACE THE WINDOW

Jan 23rd, 2008
Ankilifaly, Toliara

The view from my window looks out over a slum in one of the poorest countries of the world. Bamboo huts and tin shacks crowd the borders of a large cemetery. Old rubber tires and stones rest on tin roofs to ensure their relative security and protection during wind and rains. If I didn't look closely, I might think this was just a large garbage dump. And that's the hard part – looking beyond the filth into the eyes of these dear Malagasy people.

Something inside my soul challenges me to look beyond the poverty; look beyond the plastic buckets of water being carried from the communal tap; look beyond the naked children and into the faces of these people. With God's grace I hope to meet this challenge. I am further along in this journey than I was a few months ago. At that time, I didn't even want to look out the window. I would open the shutters and quickly turn my eyes away. It made me too sad. I just wanted to cry.

This Christmas I got a card from a friend that said, "From the humblest of places came the greatest of joys." On the front was a picture of a stable. Baby Jesus was resting in the manger. On the card was a note scratched in pen. "The view from your window is overwhelmingly sad and I am reminded that the verse in this card is still remarkably true. From the humblest of places still come the greatest of joy."

I pray that as I mature in my years of life, I learn to look beyond. Here in Madagascar, it may be to look beyond poverty. Perhaps in the States it is to look beyond a person's wealth. Maybe in war-torn countries it would be look beyond hatred and machine guns. Lord, help us to look beyond our circumstances into the eyes of Your people.

*****

Wed. Jan. 30ᵗʰ, 2008
Ankilifaly, Toliara

Praying with the Benedictines –A Window on the Cloister is a book to be read by the ordinary man/woman who desires to live a contemplative life and perhaps see some insight into monastic life. I realize these prayers might be easier to pray from the beauty of the window of the cloister. How about my view today? Can I embrace these prayers from the window (without glass panes) in the slum?

I've decided this is my assignment; God's will for my life is to embrace the window and what lies beyond.

God wants me to learn things here that I can learn no other place on this earth. Like Bonhoeffer who became better through his imprisonment and severe challenges in life I need to embrace my circumstances. God is the divine teacher and wants us to become the best in Him that we could ever be. He wants me to embrace the window.

A picture will never be able to communicate the smells and sounds outside the window. I can choose to keep my shutters closed and grope in the dark all day long. Or, I can throw them open and participate in the community around me. Black charcoal burns, overcooking the rice. The Malagasy purposefully burn their rice and drink the vitamin enriched rice water. The wind blows the stench of the neighbor's pit latrines in through my window. On a hot day it turns my stomach.

I watch young children carry buckets of water for today's cooking and bathing…women breast feeding their young… girls braiding hair…naked children playing in the dirt…the wash hanging to dry on the sticks lined as fence posts. I see my neighbors selling for a few pennies the plastic water bottles I've thrown out the previous day. In the middle of the marketplace outside my window, my neighbors begin and end their day collecting what I consider useless items to sell as merchandise in order to feed their families. Little did I know that six months later I would disciple several of these women and invite them into my home for tea.

There is no need for an alarm clock in this community. Roosters crow at 4:30 as the women light their charcoal fires to prepare the morning rice and tea. Sounds of the marketplace continue throughout the day. It is loud. The community catches a thief and beats him for punishment. I am appalled as I watch from my window. This is alien to my culture. Add to this a funeral procession. Men carry the corpse wrapped in a shroud on their shoulders, and a crowd follows chanting Malagasy songs. They walk along the narrow path to the cemetery outside my window.

This is offset by sounds which bring me joy. I hear laughter from all sides. The neighbors call out to one another throughout the day. And finally, as I rest my head upon my pillow, they sing a night-time lullaby. I hear the songs I have taught them in church, coming back to me in both English and Malagasy. What a gift God has given me through my window.

Lord, although it may at times be difficult, continue to teach me to embrace all that is beyond the window.

*****

GROWING IN OBEDIENCE

Feb. 2nd 2008
Ankilifaly, Madagascar

I cannot cling to my obedience of the past and be pleased by my obedience up to this point. Obedience is something we need to continue to grow in – a daily discipline that requires strength upon strength and daily dependence upon God and a daily working out of our salvation.

The Lord must bring us all to the point when we are willing to do only His will and to give up ourselves for the sake of His heavenly kingdom.

Lord, help me remember this as we travel back to Kenya next week and I once again see the beauty of St. Julian's Centre and what I left behind.

*****

I WILL BE WITH YOU

Feb. 17th, 2008
Nairobi, Kenya

The first evangelists ever sent to another country by the Anglican Church of Kenya were Duncan Macharia and Victor Osoro, commissioned to assist us in Madagascar. At their commissioning service at St. Luke's Anglican Church, All Saints Diocese, Bishop Todd preached on Isaiah 43: 1-2 "But now, this is what the LORD says— he who created you, O Jacob, he who formed you, O Israel: 'Fear not, for I have redeemed you; I have summoned you by name; you are mine. When you pass through the waters, I will be with you; and when you pass through the rivers, they will not sweep over you. When you walk through the fire, you will not be burned; the flames will not set you ablaze.'"

During the commissioning, I wrote the following:

I have ransomed you.
I have called you by name, you are mine.
I will be with you.
I am the Lord.
I gave a ransom.
I traded their lives.
I love you.
I am with you.

I will gather you.

I will bring my sons and daughters.

I have made them for my glory.

It was I who created them.

The I's have it!

"Even if we don't believe in God, God believes in you." -
Archbishop Desmond Tutu

*****

AM I READY?

Feb. 19th 2008, 6:30 a.m.
Rift Valley Academy, Kenya

Todd has many great plans for Madagascar although a piece
of his heart is still in Northern Kenya. When he talks to his
former students at St. Paul's, I can sense the sadness between
them – the separation and pain of transition.

And me? Am I ready? Am I ready to leave Kenya and move
on to a very different and challenging life in Madagascar? I can
only hope that by the grace of God I am ready.

So much has happened in Kenya. It has taught us our gifts,
shown us vision, caused us to grasp our ministry. It's kept
us close as a family, allowing us to see Corbi's sports games,

Charese's dramas and to be involved with our children during their high school years. By the grace of God, our missionary family has been extremely close-knit.

And now, by the grace of God, I pray that I am ready. Ready to move on to the next stage of our lives and ready to serve the Lord wherever He has us in the world.

I love you, Lord, and I pray that I am worthy to serve You all the days of my life. Amen

JUST THIS DAY

Just this day, dear Lord
I pray You give me strength.
To do the things, You've asked of me
To embrace the day at length.

To encourage the brokenhearted,
Pray for those who are weak
Feed God's people with Your Holy Word
Be humble, Courageous and meek.

To live up to the challenges You bring to me,
Not to hide my face
But with the confidence of Christ on Calvary
Walk Your path with grace.

Feb 19th, 2008, 9:30 a.m.

Rift Valley Academy, Kenya

Moving to Madagascar means a great deal of loss. It is important to note these losses as it will help in the transformational process.

Losses:

    Loss of comfort

    Loss of beauty

    Loss of immediate family being together (Corbi and Charese in college)

    Loss of extended family living together (GG and PopPop living in Kenya)

    Loss of friends

    Loss of safari

    Loss of entertainment

    Loss of grocery stores

    Loss of golf

But all the above are really nothing in contrast to surrendering to God's will and losing our lives for the sake of the gospel. Again, I am reminded of the importance of letting our own wills go and taking up our cross and following Him. I praise God for the wonderful five years we've had in Kenya and now also the opportunity to serve God once again in Madagascar. His grace is sufficient for me.

2:30 p.m.

It was a tearful goodbye to the staff of SJC. Through thick and thin we offered love and compassion to each other. Today I urged them to have strength to carry on.

"*Mahereza.*", I encouraged them, which means 'be strong,' as they say in Madagascar.

I saw Antony on the road as we were leaving today. He was riding his bike that he was able to purchase because of his job as a guard at SJC. The staff's standard of living has certainly increased over the past five years. I praise the Lord for that. Many of them have gotten married and had children, bought cell phones, bicycles, TV's and even a small car.

On my way out to the main road, I passed a flower truck exporting roses. I remembered when I first came in Jan '03. The road had a heavy grade down to the river and was impassible at times during the rainy season. Through the Redhill Community and Government officials, especially Raila Odinga, we were able to improve it – raise the level several feet – and now it is called the "Redhill Highway!" Many things can be done when we work together.

The "detour" from Madagascar has expanded my territory. It has allowed me to see and experience things I would have never been able to if I had not been on this part of the journey. Instead of only counting the "losses," I count the "gains" of being on the detour.

Gain of comfort - a 5-year comfort break

Gain of beauty – experiencing beautiful African countries, safaris and experiencing a variety of cultures!

Gain of family being together – an opportunity to be with our children in their high school years, even though they were at boarding school!

Gain of family staying in Kenya – GG and PopPop came to visit often and stayed for long periods of time ☺.

Gain of friendships.

Gain of vision and mission experience.

Gain of leadership and ministry skills.

Gain of ordination into priesthood.

Gain of others seeing our ministry in action.

Gain of trust in God and His will in our lives.

Gain of knowing God is in control.

Gain of faith…

*****

STAY BACK IN EGYPT?

Feb. 20th 2008

On the airplane from Kenya to Madagascar

Mt. Kilimanjaro can be seen for miles as we fly along the boarder of Kenya and northern Tanzania. My thoughts explode. I climbed that! I think back to the time our mission team struggled to the top, conquering our fears and persevering to the end.

I think of Joshua and Caleb who wanted to conquer the Promised Land. The others wanted to go back to Egypt where it was familiar. What would you have done if you were one of the 12 spies sent to observe the Promised Land? Would you have wanted to go forth and take possession? Or stay back in Egypt?

The option is tempting. Returning to the comfortable tent during the hard work of climbing Mt. Kilimanjaro was tempting. Desiring to stay in the comfort of Kenya is tempting as well.

Even now as I write this on the airsick sack provided by Air Madagascar, 1,200 people are left homeless and ten have died in Madagascar as a result of cyclone Ivan. But who knows about that? None of the newspapers focus on this little-known island. Oh yes, I read about the cyclone in the Kenyan paper, but only that it might hit Mozambique.

So I am wondering. Do I want to go back to Egypt? Security? Comfort? Life as I know it? Tempting, but in Egypt weren't they still in slavery? Doing it my way instead of submitting to the will of God would only put me in bondage.

My choice? Move forward. Leave behind what I know and press on into the Promised Land.

*****

OVERLOADED RICKSHAW

Feb. 21ˢᵗ 2008

Antananarivo, Madagascar

> Welcome Back to Madagascar
> My pen doesn't move
> My mind doesn't think
> My heart doesn't feel
> Because it hurts too much

All the nice ideas and spiritual thoughts I had on the plane yesterday have faded as I grasp the reality of living in Madagascar again. Staying at a friend's house in the capital, I stare at a picture on a wall. An overloaded rickshaw with sacks of rice – two men causing the rickshaw to move forward – one man pulling, the other pushing. Hard at work.

This is Malagasy life. Life is hard in Madagascar. They don't have many resources to rely on. Working together, they try to move forward, one small step at a time. The poverty even here in the capital of Antananarivo is overwhelming. I had forgotten this. After coming back from Kenya, this is even more evident. My new hometown of Toliara is even poorer than the capital. All I want to do is cry. And I do.

I feel the Spirit of God causing me to have a burden for the Malagasy people – a heart of compassion to help push the rickshaw. Before a heart can love, it first has to feel. My heart first has to break for the people with whom I am called to live.

So what am I to do as we get settled here in Madagascar? I have no goals, I have no plan. I have hopes and dreams and desires, but who knows if they will really come to fruition. I've handed these over to the Lord. He is in control and will cause these plans to prosper, if He so desires. All I have is my two small coins and I give these to the Lord. By His grace He will cause them to multiply a hundred fold, or more.

"The goal of the missionary is to do God's will, not to be useful or to win the lost. A missionary *is* useful and he *does* win the lost, but that is not his goal. His goal is to do the will of his Lord."[xlvi]

*****

I AM THEIR AMBASSADOR

I am their ambassador -
Between the rich and the poor
Bringing them to each other
And knocking on their doors
Lord grant me grace to love them
As you would have me do
To count each one with equality
And love them through and through.

*****

COMING INTO THE LIGHT

Feb. 22nd, 2008

Antananarivo, Madagascar

It always takes one's eyes time to adjust after coming into the light after groping in the darkness. That's one way I describe this culture shock that I am going through at the moment. As an American, I've come from extreme wealth, and am placed in dire poverty.

Honorine Kiplagat, our Malagasy friend living in Kenya, married to former Ambassador to France Bethuel Kiplagat, is one who can truly understand the shock and sadness of coming to Madagascar. On the night before our departure from Kenya, she had us over to her home for dinner. After a lovely evening, it was time to get some rest for the journey ahead.

"Misaotra betsaka, Tompoko," she said to me. "Many Thanks. Not many will go to Madagascar. It is a difficult country in which to work. The people are so poor. Thank you for sacrificing yourselves for the sake of the Malagasy people."

It's such an easy temptation to go forward without the Lord – to press on in our earthly duties and to leave Him behind – in the dust. What a discipline to only move as He allows. To be so sensitive to His Spirit that we move only when He moves, that we pause when He pauses, that we stop when He stops – to dance with him.

The psalmist writes it well. Ps. 143:8b, 10 "Show me the way I should go, for to you I lift up my soul... Teach me to do your will, for you are my God; may your good Spirit lead me on level ground."

*****

AT HOME IN TOLIARA

Todd and I left the capital city and returned to Toliara. Two days later we drove through the church gate and turned off the engine. I stepped out of the car and was greeted by the neighborhood children who were playing in the dirt. They called me by name and touched my skin. The priest of the local Anglican church kissed Todd's bishop's ring, and welcomed me home by shaking my hand. "*Tonga soa.*" (Welcome.) We were surrounded by a flock of parishioners within seconds.

Pierre, our guard, took our luggage and followed us up the stairs. His wife, Jeannette had unlocked the door and opened the windows, anticipating our arrival. As I climbed the stairs I saw a familiar face that brought me joy. Nolavy was cooking outside her house down below. As she looked up, her face broke into a smile. Her compassionate spirit welcomed me home.

The realization had come to me. It is because of people like Nolavy that I am in Toliara. She is the daughter of a local priest of the African Traditional Religion. At 20 years old she is studying to pass her high school degree. She has two more years to finish.

Our eyes connected and I realized here was my purpose. It was for women like Nolavy that I had come back to Madagascar. My detour was complete.

*****

END OF CONSTRUCTION
THANK YOU FOR YOUR PATIENCE[xlvii]

The epitaph on Ruth Bell Graham's tombstone reads: "End of Construction. Thank you for your patience." I have followed the detour signs and have once again arrived in Madagascar. As long as we are on this earth, our construction is without end. When we journey with God, our off-road safari is never boring.

Following God's path does not always come easily, nor naturally, but it is a learned obedience. Much like a painter who has learned her primary skills in first grade art, she later develops the elementary basics. Our journey is one of growth and transformation. As we journey through time we mature. Growing in knowledge and understanding our obedience is perfected and we learn to follow Christ more naturally, or rather supernaturally. May people have patience with us along the way.

LESSONS LEARNED ALONG THE DETOUR:

I realize God is using the past to prepare us for future endeavors and is causing me to live a life worthy of the calling I have received. (Eph. 4:1) He is giving me direction as He reveals His plans for us in Toliara, Madagascar. What does the Lord require of us? We are brought into this life to act justly, love mercy and walk humbly with our God. (Micah 6:8)

DETOUR PRAYER:

Dear Lord, You have told us in Your Word that our life is the width of our hand and is just a moment to you; human existence is but a breath. (Ps. 39:5) We are guests in God's world –travelers passing through, as our ancestors were before us. (Ps. 39:12) Teach me to look outside the window and into the heart of your people. Help me to reach out beyond myself to others in love, holding my neighbors' hands along the way, all the while remembering; "In his heart a man plans his course, but the LORD determines his steps. (Proverbs 16:9) In Jesus' Name. Amen.

I welcome you to stay connected with our ministry, *People Reaching People*, by visiting our website, www.peoplereaching.org. The website is full of information regarding our ministry activities, our monthly calendar, recent newsletters, prayer requests and includes an extensive photo gallery. It also contains information on how to order my first book, *A Guest in God's World: Memories of Madagascar* and allows you to write us or support us on the mission field through the "contact us" section. Enjoy!

Bibliography

Benner, David. *Sacred Companions: The Gift of Spiritual Friendship & Direction.* Downers Grove: InterVarsity Press, 2004. Print.

Chambers, Oswald. *My Utmost for His Highest.* Grand Rapids: Discovery House, 2008. Print.

Coleman, Robert E. *The Master's Way of Personal Evangelism.* Wheaton, Crossway Books, 1997. Print.

Eggerichs, Emerson. *Love & Respect: The Love She Most Desires; The Respect He Desperately Needs.* Franklin: Integrity Publishers, 2004. Print.

Elliot, Elisabeth. *Through Gates of Splendor.* Wheaton: Tyndale House Publishers, 1975. Print.

Ford, Kevin. *Transforming Church: Bringing Out the Good to Get to Great.* Nashville: David C. Cook, 2008. Print.

Foster, Richard J. *Devotional Classics: Revised Edition-Selected Readings for Individuals and Groups.* New York: HarperOne, 2005. Print.

Graham, Ruth Bell. *Footprints of a Pilgrim.* Nashville: Thomas Nelson, 2001. Print.

Kirby, Scott. *Equipped for Adventure: A Practical Guide to Short-Term Mission Trips.* Birmingham: New Hope Publishers, 2006. Print.

Littleton, Mark R. *"The New Footprints"; Escaping the Time Crunch.* Chicago: Moody Press, 1990. Print.

Maxwell, John C. *Running with the Giants: What the Old Testament Heroes Want You to Know About Life and Leadership.* Brentwood: FaithWords, 2002. Print.

Maxwell, John C. *Thinking for a Change: 11 Ways Highly Successful People Approach Life and Work.* Nashville: Center Street, 2005. Print.

Ortberg, John. *The Life You've Always Wanted: Spiritual Disciplines for Ordinary People.* Grand Rapids: Zondervan, 2002. Print.

Parker, Rebecca Ann. *Proverbs of Ashes: Violence, Redemptive Suffering, and the Search for What Saves Us.* Boston: Beacon Press, 2002. Print.

Rubietta, Jane. *Resting Place: A Personal Guide to Spiritual Retreats.* Downers Grove: InterVarsity Press, 2006. Print.

Rumford, Douglas J. *SoulShaping: Taking Care of Your Spiritual Life.* Wheaton: Tyndale House Publishers, Inc., 2001. Print.

Thomas, Gary. *Sacred Pathways.* Grand Rapids: Zondervan, 2002. Print.

Warren, Rick. *The Purpose Driven Life: What on Earth Am I Here For?* Grand Rapids: Zondervan, 2007. Print.

Wong, David W.F. *Journeys Beyond the Comfort Zone.* Kihei: Haggai Institute, 2002. Print.

i   Rebecca Ann Parker, *Proverbs of Ashes: Violence, Redemptive Suffering, and the Search for What Saves Us.*

ii   Kevin Ford, *Transforming Church: Bringing Out the Good to Get to Great,* 176.

iii   Kevin Ford, *Transforming Church: Bringing Out the Good to Get to Great,* 166.

iv   E. Stanley Jones.

v   Richard Foster, *Devotional Classics,* 451.

vi   John Maxwell, *Thinking for a Change: 11 Ways Highly Successful People Approach Life and Work,* 35.

vii   John Maxwell, *Thinking for a Change: 11 Ways Highly Successful People Approach Life and Work,* 34.

viii   John Maxwell, *Thinking for a Change: 11 Ways Highly Successful People Approach Life and Work,* 35.

ix   John Maxwell, *Thinking for a Change: 11 Ways Highly Successful People Approach Life and Work.*

x   John Maxwell, *Thinking for a Change: 11 Ways Highly Successful People Approach Life and Work,* 175.

xi   Jane Rubietta, *Resting Place, A Personal Guide to Spiritual Retreats,* 69.

xii   Jane Rubietta, *Resting Place, A Personal Guide to Spiritual Retreats,* 69.

xiii   Jane Rubietta, *Resting Place, A Personal Guide to Spiritual Retreats,* 69.

xiv   Jane Rubietta, *Resting Place, A Personal Guide to Spiritual Retreats,* 69.

xv   David Benner, *Spiritual Companions: The Gift of Spiritual Friendship & Direction,* 84.

xvi   Elisabeth Elliot, *Through the Gates of Splendor,* Epilogue II.

xvii   Elisabeth Elliot, *Through the Gates of Splendor,* 270.

xviii   Elisabeth Elliot, *Through the Gates of Splendor,* 14.

xix   Elisabeth Elliot, *Through the Gates of Splendor,* 22.

xx   Elisabeth Elliot, *Through the Gates of Splendor,* 14.

xxi   Elisabeth Elliot, *Through the Gates of Splendor,* 29.

xxii   Elisabeth Elliot, *Through the Gates of Splendor,* 31.

xxiii   Elisabeth Elliot, *Through the Gates of Splendor,* 56.

xxiv   Elisabeth Elliot, *Through the Gates of Splendor,* 60.

xxv   Elisabeth Elliot, *Through the Gates of Splendor,* 151.

xxvi   Elisabeth Elliot, *Through the Gates of Splendor,* 20.

xxvii   Scott Kirby, *Equipped for Adventure: A Practical Guide to Short-Term Mission Trips,* Back Cover.

xxviii   Scott Kirby, *Equipped for Adventure: A Practical Guide to Short-Term Mission Trips,* 30.

*****

LaVergne, TN USA
08 April 2010
178615LV00003B/2/P